SPORT
IMAGES

FIRST EDITION, FIRST PRINTING January 2006


SPORT IMAGES, TRUCKEE, CALIFORNIA, USA

www.sportimages.com

TEXT & PHOTOGHRAPHY COPYRIGHT ©2006 BY UDO MACHAT

PRINTED IN CHINA by EVERBEST PRINTING
ISBN 0-9618712-9-6

# Golf Courses of the
# High Sierra

A Sport Images Book *by* Udo Machat

*It was by luck*

*that I was introduced to golf....*

*and I'll be forever grateful*

*to those who gave me*

*that luck.*

# Contents

# The High Sierra

THE SIERRA NEVADA IS A FOUR HUNDRED AND THIRTY mile-long colossus, a giant piece of the earth's crust between fifty and eighty miles wide, soaring to a height of almost fifteen thousand feet. It is a piece of nature covering many themes and prompting superlatives that only Californians can comfortably fit into their everyday vernacular. The Sierra Nevada has the largest trees, the deepest canyons, the most snow, the highest waterfalls, the highest mountain peak in the lower forty-eight, the oldest National Park and the richest gold finds. And its snow run-off keeps a grateful population fed. It is a mountain range that is one piece of continuous granite, slightly tilted to the east, resulting in an escarpment that is almost perpendicular to the flat desert floor below. In the west it takes a more leisurely trip to its ultimate height, resulting in rolling foothills covered by thick forests, gurgling streams and meadows.

The High Sierra visible today is about five million years old, though the evolution can be traced back to about five hundred million years. The most significant occurrence in creating the Sierra Nevada came when the Pacific Plate pushed under the North American Plate. This was two hundred and fifty million years ago. A more recent earthquake, in 1872, increased the height of the Sierra Nevada by about twenty feet and also

bumped it sideways by about forty. This earthquake decimated the town of Lone Pine, killing several dozen people.

The Sierra Nevada was inadvertently named by a Spaniard in 1776, when he described it as "una gran sierra nevada" or "Snowy Range." Though a few individual explorers and mountain men crossed the Sierra Nevada in search of trade and trade routes, it wasn't until 1844 that a party of fifty people set out from Council Bluffs, Idaho, to seek a better life in California. They succeeded in scaling the Sierra Nevada with the help of a chief of the Paiute Indian Nation. The emigrants mistakenly thought his name to be Truckee, since he often answered ques-

tions with a word that sounded like that. In fact, "truk-eee" is a Paiute word meaning "all right."

Today the trip from Truckee to Reno takes about half an hour along a four-lane highway. In 1844 the progress by these emigrants, urging their cattle up the steep canyon, not knowing whether their journey would result in ultimate success, was measured in yards per hour rather than today's miles per hour. If you envision the Truckee river canyon today without the smooth, massive roadway, what remains are large boulders, the river cascading down the slope, obstacles piled upon obstacles. One can only marvel at the determination of the people of that time. Or, perhaps wonder how bad their situation was where they came from.

The highest point in the Sierra Nevada is Mount Whitney, which rises to almost 14,700 feet toward the southern extremity of this mountain range. In the north, the highest point is Mount Shasta, 14,400 feet high. Approximately halfway between these giants is the world renowned Yosemite National Park. This park was founded by an Act of Congress in 1890 due in large part to the lobbying efforts of John Muir, earning him recognition as the "Father of Our National Park System."

John Muir was born in Scotland on April 21, 1838, and came to America at the age of eleven. His family settled in Wisconsin, where he helped farm the land. During this time he fell in love with nature and also became something of an inventor, as well as a traveler with a deep seated curiosity. In 1868 he would see the Sierra Nevada for the first time, and it was love at first sight. He settled in Yosemite, staying for four years, herded sheep and inadvertently started his career as a writer. He would eventually write about 300 articles and publish ten books that would address his travels and the infant environmental movement. He along with some of his like-minded supporters founded the Sierra Club in 1892, saying: "Do something

for wilderness and make the mountains glad."

Another man whose creative genius is indelibly linked to the Sierra Nevada, and Yosemite National Park in particular, is Ansel Adams. He was born in San Francisco in 1902, discovered the camera and Yosemite in 1916 and until his death in 1984 returned every year to the high country. He was an environmentalist, a very active member of the Sierra Club and, as John Muir before him, an outspoken advocate for wilderness. His black and white images of Half Dome and El Capitan captured the imagination of all who saw them, and he arguably became the eyes through which Americans saw wilderness.

Weather in the Sierra Nevada can be extreme. Summers, though, are moderate, usually with hardly a cloud to be seen. With almost no measurable precipitation for months on end, there is always the danger of fire from the occasional lightning storm. Spring and fall can be shortened considerably by early and late snowfalls. In 2004, spring was about a week long because winter didn't want to give up its hold. Fall is just about the most beautiful and bracing time to be in the Sierra. The air is cleaner and fresher, the aspens add a colorful new dimension to the evergreens, and everyone and everything gets ready for the first snow, which usually makes its grand entrance in the middle of October. Winter is extreme in the Sierra; snowfalls of ten to twelve feet in one sitting are not too unusual. But when there are accumulations of only three or four feet, life goes on without missing a beat. It's a wonderful time.

The California Geological Survey first defined the term "High Sierra" in 1864. It was decided that the part of the Sierra Nevada that is above the tree line, from the tops of the highest peaks down to about nine or ten thousand feet would be called High Sierra. However, for the purpose of this book we decided that our definition of High Sierra is more a state of mind and extended it downward into the forest to an altitude of about five thousand feet.

Many a man and woman, me included, have fallen for the charms of this unique mountain range. We thank all of them for being responsible in their use of this resource. And none should be thanked more than the man who initiated the process, the man who had the foresight and made it his life's work to ensure that the Sierra Nevada could remain as pristine as is possible, considering the many thousands who come to visit each and every year.

John Muir, we thank you for that.

# Introduction

SPORT AND RECREATION HAS LONG BEEN ASSOCIATED with the High Sierra. In the early years the main activity was limited to hiking along animal trails and marveling at the majestic scenery. During the winter months, the Sierra Nevada slept and recovered from these several dozen hikers.

Today, activities are slightly more diverse. During the winter there is downhill skiing, cross-country skiing, snow boarding, snow shoeing and ice skating; as far as I know there is no ice fishing. In the summer there is water skiing, swimming, wave boarding, backpacking, rock climbing, trail running, fishing, soaring and even ballooning....well, you get the idea. And before I forget, there is golf. Now there are approximately thirty golf courses of various sizes and descriptions. It hasn't always been that way.

The first few golf courses in the Sierra Nevada opened for play in the early twenties on the north shore of Lake Tahoe. Now there are golf courses from the Feather River in the north to Mammoth Lakes in the south.

Golf has changed from a game where you played, perhaps competed, enjoyed the out-of-doors, appreciated the smell of the cut grass as well as the sound of birds and the wind in the trees—the little things, the accents. It has changed from that to a lifestyle, with homes alongside fairways, with country clubs that are indeed in the country, with gated communities away from the realities of life. Nevertheless, one quality that has remained the same in golf is that of individual achievement. There are two men who through their individual efforts, their dogged determination and their love for the Sierra have made it possible for thousands to enjoy new ways of recreation.

Dave McCoy had visited the Mammoth area as a youngster, was an accomplished competitive skier and owned a portable rope tow for skiers that he would move around to where the best snow was. This was in the years around 1940. What he discovered was that the best snow was consistently found on the north facing slope of Mammoth Mountain. The U.S. Forest Service wanted more ski areas built and developed and put Mammoth Mountain up for bid. There were no takers. The thinking was that there was too much snow. McCoy, who had a relationship with the Forest Service but no money, was awarded the property by default. He lived up to the challenge.

Alexander Cushing had the audacity to apply to the International Olympic Committee to hold the 1960 winter event in Squaw Valley. At the time this now world-famous ski resort had one chair lift, two rope tows and a lodge with fifty rooms—no infrastructure, no buildings for the various events and the athletes, and no highways. It was hardly a place for a huge international event. By a vote of thirty-two to thirty his bid was chosen over Austria's Innsbruck. His winning theme for the presentation was: "A return to the Olympic ideals of simplicity with a focus on athleticism and diversity." Cushing pushed to get the facilities in place, the event was a huge success, and Squaw Valley has built on that success since. It seems it pays to have audacity.

The reason these two men are important to this book about golf courses, and worthy of mention, is that they made the Sierra Nevada a destination recognized internationally. Within the United States and in California especially, it became an accepted vacation area. It took this larger-than-life public relations effort to bring the number of people to the High Sierra necessary to support these courses.

The photography for this book, with just the very odd exception, was done in September 2005. At that time, the snow on the highest peaks had just recently melted, and the fall foliage had not yet begun to turn color. Since the photography had to be accomplished before the golf courses closed for the season, this was a condition we had to accept.

*UDO MACHAT*
*Truckee, California, October 2005*

FAR FROM THE HECTIC, NON-STOP PACE OF THE city, far from the crowded streets ruled by machines and driven people, is another world, the idyllic countryside of the Sierra Nevada foothills in the Feather River valley. It was an easy and apt choice for the site of the Grizzly Ranch Club. The closest town is Portola, a non-descript hamlet with not one four-star establishment in sight. And that's just the way Grizzly's members like it. The solitude, the remoteness, is not an illusion. It's as real as the beauty of the landscape in this tranquil place.

The charm and beauty of the area did not escape the attention of land developer Andy Norris, who saw the remoteness of this area as a benefit, not a liability. He attracted some investors who purchased eleven hundred acres of a larger ranch that extended all the way to the Feather River and beyond. The group of fourteen investors became known as "the Founders." Andy Norris then pulled together a team to put on paper his vision of a real estate development built around a golf course that "fit the land."

# Grizzly Ranch Club

*7,411 yards, par 72*

*Architect: Robert Cupp*

*Opened for play: September 2005*

*Altitude: 5,164 feet*

*Head Professional: Matt Magnotta*

THE NINTH HOLE, A DOWNHILL 439-YARD PAR-FOUR
SHOWN AT RIGHT FROM THE WHITE TEES AND A CLOSER LOOK
OF ITS GREEN, ABOVE

This included Gage Davis an architect and land planner from Scottsdale, Robert Cupp who would design the golf course, and Jack Bridge who had an intimate knowledge of the land. Bridge had been instrumental in the real estate planning and is still active as a design consultant to the project. A few of the Founders had an association with Lowe Enterprises, Andy Norris headed their Resort and Hotel division, so it was of no surprise that Lowe Enterprises became involved, had the clout to procure the financing and then became the developers of Grizzly Ranch Club. A project so obviously focused on quality would fit very nicely into their ever expanding portfolio.

Lowe Enterprises has worked hard over the last thirty-three years to build a reputation based on quality. It is a privately owned corporation that is active in the management and development of hospitality properties. Destination Development Corporation, a subsidiary of Lowe Enterprises, specializes in the development of hotels and golf courses.

The course takes full advantage of the natural topography. It curls back and forth in the valleys and plains that are heavily forested with ponderosa pine and permanently preserved wetlands. The peaks of the High Sierra are all around, adding their snow-capped beauty. Quite often these peaks are at the center of a perfectly designed composition. The fourth green, with forest on both sides, and a mountain peak in the distance, is an excellent example of what now might be thought of as a happy conincidence, but was actually accomplished with much thought at the routing stage.

Grizzly Ranch examines all aspects of your game, careful strategy as well as execution. Four sets of tees give a group with differing abilities the chance to enjoy a round together, only occasionally making weaker players weep.

Just a few hundred yards from the first tee and adjacent to the eighteenth green is a large practice area that is destined to become the social hub of the golf course. There is a generous driving range that can accommodate about thirty golfers at a time, there is a sand bunker with a green to practice those pesky explosion shots, and there is a putting green to get the speed just right. Then there is the Lake House, convenient for a snack half-way through the round or to relax with friends after the round and watch other groups negotiate the eighteenth. All this activity happens just below the golf shop that presides over all this. Matt enjoys keeping an eye on his flock from his perch high above.

Matt Magnotta is the head professional at Grizzly Ranch.

*OVERLEAF:*
*THE FINISHING HOLE IN ALL ITS GLORY*

THE SEVENTEENTH HOLE, HAS A CREEK FIRST RUNNING ACROSS AND THEN ON THE LEFT SIDE OF THE FAIRWAY

As many others who came to live in the High Sierra, it was the snow and skiing that was the magnet. His first winter in Tahoe he worked at Squaw Valley as a ski instructor. In golf he had various positions, starting with caddying in his youth, to becoming head professional at The Dragon, and finally culminating with his present position at Grizzly Ranch Club.

It was a good idea to make the warm-up area prominent, because your game will need to be in high gear before the first shot of the round. The first hole starts out with a bang. Standing on the teeing ground, you won't quite be able to see the green, but you will see a heart-shaped bunker on the left side of the fairway to aim at and a sea of natural grasses that has to be carried. The hole is 436 yards long, a par-four with a gently undulating fairway that is on a slight oblique to your tee shot, making a slight draw a very good thing. There are two bunkers left of the green, one small, one large, quite possibly saving your ball from bounding into doom.

The second hole is a par-three of 179 yards. The green, beautifully framed by the forest, is not too deep but is quite wide. The left half of the green is protected by a bunker, leaving the right side open. In its native state, the forest was quite a bit more dense, but it was thinned to make it look less threatening and to allow light to filter down to the ground.

The first par-five is the third, which is 640 yards long and plays slightly uphill, cresting 275 yards from the tee. There is not much of a danger of anyone getting to the green in two, but on the off chance someone should try, the fairway ends a little more than a hundred yards short of the green and is replaced by a wetlands, which some golfers will find quite challenging to carry. Utter doom is what you would face from there. The green has two bunkers in front and one behind and is one of the easier greens to putt. If you're close that is.

The fourth is a par-four 473 yards long, a dogleg right with a quite dramatic tee shot to an uphill fairway that seemingly starts a mile away. The second shot is to a green in one of the more beautiful settings on the course. It is guarded by two bunkers on the right, leaving an opening for a running approach, which on this hole will be common. Number five is another lengthy par-four at 451 yards. The tee shot has to be directed at a fairway that is bordered by wetlands, and with a successful drive there should only be a middle-iron shot left to a green that is completely open in front, but does have a trap on the left, and one behind.

Number six is a monstrous par-three of 237 yards.

*SAND HAZARDS ON THE SIXTH HOLE, TOP, AND AT THE EIGHTH, BOTTOM*

However, the green is quite large and has an apron leading to the putting surface should your shot be a bit short, which many will be. There are four bunkers on the right side, with the green curving in behind the closest one. A flag placed behind this bunker might even challenge Tiger Woods.

The seventh hole is a short par-five measuring 517 yards. The fairway has no bunkers and is in a straight line from tee to green. It pinches in slightly for the extremely long hitters, but opens up again short of the green, which has a very prominent bunker at the front-center. There are two plateaus, making for some interesting putting lines should you be on the wrong tier.

The eighth is a par-four, 421 yards long. There is nothing clandestine or devious about this hole. The fairway is inviting, and two good, crisp shots to a green that only has one bunker close by, should provide ample satisfaction.

Of all the spectacular scenes on this course, the ninth, a par-four, 439 yards long, offers perhaps the most spectacular. From an elevated tee, the fairway runs downhill and curves across the line of the shot. The green is placed beside a lake, but with a little foresight should not pose a real problem. Beckwourth Peak is dominant over the middle of the green in the distance. This hole is what golf is about. It has visual beauty and the chance

*THE OPENING HOLE WITH ITS GREEN HIDDEN BEHIND A WALL OF PINE ON THE LEFT*

*NUMBER TWELVE*

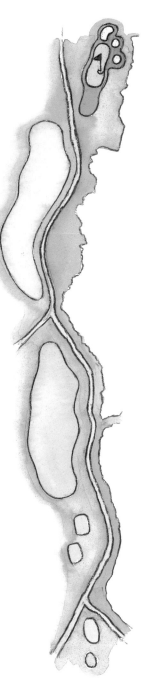

to excel in the execution.

Number ten, a 433-yard par-four, starts the back nine in a slightly different mode. The fairway rises from the tee, with a single pot bunker providing direction. The hole doglegs to the left, forcing a second shot over rough. There are no bunkers at the green, but a grass hollow on the left side will pose problems for the second shot. The next hole, also a par-four, gives the long hitter a chance to get home from the tee. It is a mere 318 yards long and, as short par-fours should, offers several approaches. Some players can attempt to drive the green, but most should be using a mid- to long iron. A little pot bunker, exactly in the middle front, seems to be part of the green.

The twelfth is a man-sized par-five, 649 yards long and starting downhill to the first of two fairway areas that are separated by a brook. From the tee this brook is partly hidden, the growth in the river bed only appearing to pinch in from both sides. The second landing area makes a turn to the right, and is again interrupted by the same brook, one that doesn't seem to be able to make up its mind which way to go. The green, about thirty yards beyond the brook, is a little above the fairway and is narrow and long. This third shot into a gorgeous setting should be enjoyed. Only the strongest can expect to have a real-

NUMBER FOURTEEN
A 217-YARD PAR-THREE

*THE FOURTH GREEN*

*THE DOGLEG AT NUMBER FOUR, A 473-YARD PAR-FOUR*

istic chance of reaching the green in two. But of course that's no reason to not attempt it.

Number thirteen, is an uphill, out-in-the-open par-four, 460 yards long. The fairway is wide and inviting, with several smallish bunkers on the right side. There is a false front on a large green, the natural terrain rising quite steeply behind.

The fourteenth is a 217-yard par-three. It is situated on the highest part of the property in a stunning setting, with trees behind the green and bunkers on the right and behind. Late in the day, with the sun filtering through the trees, it is especially a sight to be cherished.

Number fifteen is a short par-four of 330 yards. It has a very wide, inviting fairway, but the opening to the green is extremely narrow. The sixteenth is only 167 yards long, a par-three from highly elevated tees. The front edge of the green is defined by a wetland, and there are two small bunkers behind the green that don't really come into play. Number seventeen is a par-four 483 yards long and an exceptionally appealing hole.

The fairway is cut in half by a creek that produces a ten-foot deep and fifteen-yard wide depression that can possibly be reached from the tee but must be avoided at all cost. The creek then continues down the left side, all the way to the green.

The finishing hole is a par-five of 570 yards. Golfers are a shifty lot, some preferring to give their approval only to the seemingly tough, the dramatically clothed but easily conquered. This golf hole is tough, does not hide behind a facade, and satisfies all the criteria that make a golf hole great. On the right there is rough and a creek that then cuts across the fairway and into a lake that stretches all the way to the green. Offering many opportunities for drama, the hole has to be well understood and precisely played. Great hole, great golf course.

And who created this oasis in the northernmost reaches of the Sierra Nevada? There is no simple answer….there were a lot of individuals who over a long period of time in many differing disciplines shaped and molded the outward skin of this impressive place. However, the person who gets full credit for the design of the golf course is Robert Cupp.

He is a man of many talents, many interests and quite a few passions with the ability that creative people have to have. The ability to visualize the finished product well in advance of its conclusion. In his so-called formative years his career direction was toward the fine arts, making a meager living as a portraitist and then working for advertising agencies. He had always been athletic, with a special love for golf. Eventually the two disciplines merged, resulting in some small design jobs at local golf courses. This led to his return to school, and a degree in agronomy and a position with Nicklaus Design, where he stayed for fifteen years. He opened his own firm in 1984.

Some of the golf courses Robert Cupp has lent his special talents to are both courses at Pumpkin Ridge in Oregon, Big Sky in British Columbia, Starr Pass in Arizona. And closer to his office in Georgia there is Druid Hills, Hawks Ridge and The Links at Savannah Harbor. And north of the border in Toronto, he forged Beacon Hall. All in all he is responsible for creating in excess of one hundred golf courses, eleven of these winning Best New Course awards.

Cupp thoroughly enjoys designing greens. The initial design happens at the computer with the final tweaking done in the field with hard hat in place. His greens can present any number of problems to the complacent player. They can have subtle breaks, most are multi-tiered allowing for several pin positions and some of the greens have false fronts presenting a very nice target from the fairway. They have only one commonality. They have nothing in common.

When he first toured the property of what was to become Grizzly Ranch, Cupp said: "When I first saw the land, it immediately brought to mind Castle Pines. It has the same topography, the same elevation, same slope, same soil and the same understory—the forested areas along each fairway that are open enough to let you walk around. I couldn't believe my good fortune when I saw what I had to work with."

| Hole | 1 | 2 | 3 | 4 | 5 | 6 | 7 | 8 | 9 | Out | | 10 | 11 | 12 | 13 | 14 | 15 | 16 | 17 | 18 | In | Tot | Hcp | Net |
|---|---|---|---|---|---|---|---|---|---|---|---|---|---|---|---|---|---|---|---|---|---|---|---|---|
| Black | 436 | 179 | 640 | 473 | 451 | 237 | 517 | 421 | 439 | 3793 | I N I T I A L | 433 | 318 | 649 | 460 | 217 | 330 | 158 | 483 | 570 | 3618 | 7411 | | |
| Green | 398 | 166 | 599 | 452 | 411 | 205 | 492 | 389 | 399 | 3511 | | 375 | 267 | 621 | 430 | 186 | 301 | 139 | 425 | 527 | 3271 | 6782 | | |
| White | 338 | 138 | 557 | 356 | 366 | 166 | 455 | 339 | 355 | 3070 | | 338 | 235 | 546 | 402 | 156 | 266 | 134 | 389 | 488 | 2954 | 6024 | | |
| Men's Hcp | 13 | 17 | 1 | 3 | 7 | 9 | 11 | 15 | 5 | | | 10 | 18 | 2 | 6 | 12 | 14 | 16 | 8 | 4 | | | | |
| | | | | | | | | | | | | | | | | | | | | | | | | |
| Par | 4 | 3 | 5 | 4 | 4 | 3 | 5 | 4 | 4 | 36 | | 4 | 4 | 5 | 4 | 3 | 4 | 3 | 4 | 5 | 36 | | | |
| | | | | | | | | | | | | | | | | | | | | | | | | |
| Ladies' Hcp | 5 | 17 | 1 | 3 | 7 | 9 | 13 | 15 | 11 | | | 12 | 18 | 2 | 10 | 14 | 6 | 16 | 8 | 4 | | | | |
| Red | 302 | 106 | 504 | 321 | 322 | 132 | 436 | 308 | 319 | 2750 | | 309 | 208 | 512 | 361 | 116 | 241 | 117 | 349 | 448 | 2661 | 5411 | | |

Date:      Scorer:            Attest:

# The Dragon at Gold Mountain

*7,077 yards, par 72*

*Architect: Robin Nelson*

*Opened for play: 2000*

*Altitude: 5,052 feet*

*Head Professional: Joe Lietch*

THERE'S ONE THING ABOUT THE GARNERS—NO one will ever accuse them of not seeing the big picture. Peggy and Dariel Garner were touring the country in their Bronco, searching for a place to purchase on which they could enjoy their golden years. After many thousands of miles, they happened onto Gold Mountain, an area at the northernmost tip of the Sierra Nevada, nestled against the Feather River. They purchased 1,280 acres, found an architect, decided it was too much land for a single house, but quickly formulated a plan to build a golf course and develop parts of the remaining property into a variety of upscale home sites. The plan was so sound and appealing that the permits were in place in a little more than a year and construction of the golf course and the marketing of the home sites could begin.

The man chosen to design the golf course was Robin Nelson, whose architectural philosophy as well

*NUMBER SEVENTEEN, A 175-YARD PAR-THREE*

as his environmental sensitivity mirrored the ones held by the Garners. Nelson has a solid knowledge of all the disciplines and holds all the appropriate degrees to qualify as one of the top golf architects practicing today. He has designed well over one hundred courses around the world, including Mauna Lani in Hawaii. Says Nelson about The Dragon: "The golf course follows the natural contours of the setting, the Feather River Canyon, which is where the real architecture is, allowing the course to flow over the site. We didn't do any landscaping. We didn't introduce any plants at all. So what was there is still there." Many architects strive to make their designs blend into the natural setting. This approach of using what Mother Nature supplied gratis is quite novel.

The clubhouse overlooking the course is also quite novel. Nakoma Country Club in Madison, Wisconsin, had once retained Frank Lloyd Wright to design the clubhouse for their newly formed club. For various reasons—money may have had something to do with it—the clubhouse was never built, although the plans were completed. The plans became part of Wright's archives, and after his death they were stored and preserved by his foundation. The Garner's found out about this through Taliesin Architects, whose expertise they had employed

before, the continuation of Wright's practice, and retained them to oversee construction of the clubhouse as well as some of the residences. Nakoma, as the clubhouse was named, now houses the pro shop, a spa and restaurant. The clubhouse has been called "the most unique building of its kind in America," with five spires reminiscent of Indian teepees, and I agree. It dominates the landscape and is well worth studying, inside and out.

On the last Saturday in May 2000, as part of the official opening, The Dragon golf course was blessed by Taoist priests. The blessing was to consecrate the ground and free all the captive spirits, returning them to heaven. This awakening ceremony included the soothing sounds of flutes and drums, and featured the awakening dance of three mystical lions named "Fu Dogs." This dance was performed by Tao Kung Moon.

"Send me your heroes," is a tag line written by Peggy and Dariel that succinctly describes players who bravely march to the back tees. Through Peggy's involvement, women playing the course are also given a chance, with thoughtfully placed forward tees, to be heroic while still enjoying their round. Patty Sheehan, a Ladies Professional Golf Association legend, came on board to work with Nelson to ensure that women were served well in his design.

*THE EIGHTEENTH GREEN, SURROUNDED BY PROTECTIVE BUNKERS*

NUMBER SIX, ABOVE, LOOKING BACK TO THE DOGLEG AND ACROSS THE INTIMIDATING BARRANCA

NEXT PAGE, TOP: THE VIEW FROM THE TEE AT NUMBER FIFTEEN AND THE TRAPS AT NUMBER THREE BELOW

This championship course, a little longer than seven thousand yards, winds its way through valleys and crests of the gently contoured foothills of the Sierra Nevada. Fully taking advantage of natural features, adding a few bunkers and choosing tee sites and places for greens, it seems that no design work was done. Or done so well it can't be seen. As the golf course took shape, it became apparent that all holes had their own individual personality deserving a name. As a result, each hole beside a number was given a thought provoking name.

Standing on the first tee, driver at the ready, will surely raise your blood pressure by a point or two. There is something disconcerting about a golf hole that rather unabashedly reveals all its secrets so easily. *Dragon's Lookout*, is a 533-yard par-five that somehow seems longer. The tee shot should be hit toward the left side, the second toward a bunker on the right. This will reveal an opening between trees to the green, which is sloped from left to right and demands that the ball be kept short of the hole location.

Number two, *Deception*, is 458 yards long, a lengthy par-four that needs a straight drive that has to be played far enough to see the green located beyond an entrenchment about thirty-five feet below the fairway. There is a bunker short and left of

*OVERLEAF:*
*THE OPENING HOLE, A PRECURSOR OF WHAT'S TO COME*

NAKOMA, THE FRANK LLOYD WRIGHT DESIGNED CLUBHOUSE

the green and two sizable traps on the right.

Number three, *Simplicity*, is 400 yards long but plays shorter from an elevated tee. The second shot is a bit uphill to a green that has two bunkers front and left. The shape of the traps is interesting, resembling ancient symbols; perhaps a message is encrypted? Keeping the ball below the hole will be to your benefit.

The fourth hole, appropriately named *Faith*, is a 320-yard par-four of the risk-reward variety. To the left side of the fairway is the Feather River canyon. The hole can be played a number of ways, but all lead to a small, well-bunkered

green. To hold the green, a high shot is imperative.

The greens on The Dragon, all one hundred thousand square feet of them, are seeded in creeping bent. Most greens are guarded by bunkers that have interesting shapes, are undulating, the majority with several plateaus. Some bunkers have faces that are quite steep, and some have the secondary duty of catching your ball before it bounds into an unplayable situation. The bunkers short of the fourth green are a good example. The fairways are Misty Chateau bluegrasss which needs little water and responds well to environmentally friendly fertilizers.

Number five, *Hope*, is a par-three 164 yards long. The green is the smallest on the golf course, so hitting it will give you a realistic attempt at birdie. The tees, all six, demonstrate how differently the golf course can play from the various places. There is a one hundred yard difference from the front to back tees on this hole.

Number six, *Charity*, is 456 yards long. It is a dogleg to the left, tempting you to gain a little advantage by drawing the ball close to the left side. That's probably a bad idea. The bunker visible from the tee is the aim, setting up a second shot that might be a little longer than the first. The green, quite wide and not too deep, is fronted by a small bunker.

Number seven, *Dragon's Tail*, is a 499-yard par-five. The fairway tilts from left to right, favoring a shot over the fairway bunker on the left side. The second shot is slightly downhill, with a lake to the left of the green. The green itself is elevated and has been misread by many. Be careful.

The eighth hole, *Looking Glass*, is a par-three of 192 yards. The tee shot has to navigate a pond that stretches most of the way to the green. This is a great hole, with bunkers on both sides and a smaller one behind the green. Par on this hole is to be commended. Number nine, *Perseverance*, is 398 yards long. A tee shot to the left center will be good. The approach to the green is narrow, between two traps with steep faces. Going long over this green is doom.

Starting the back nine, *Dragon's Lagoon*, is downhill, 433 yards long. The trap on the right should not be in play, but a drive right over it will put you in ideal position for your second. But be careful—the green has a pond to the left and two small bunkers on the right. The eleventh, *Teeth of the Dragon*, is a 553-yard par-five. The tee shot needs to follow the shape of the narrow fairway, which turns and slants to the right and discourages the use of driver off the tee. Usually then, it is not reachable in

THE INFAMOUS, SHORT PAR-FOUR FOURTH HOLE
FROM A FORWARD TEE

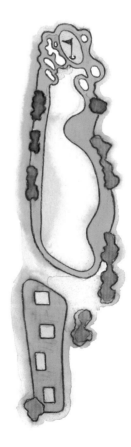

STRATEGICALLY PLACED BUNKERS GUARD THE SECOND GREEN ABOVE, AND
VARIOUS SHAPES OF BUNKERS AT RIGHT

two. The second shot might be a 3 or 4-iron, with a wedge to the green. The twelfth, *Dragon's Gate*, has been called one of the all-time best golf holes by the United States Golf Association's Golf Journal. That's quite an accolade, but should par be achieved you might just agree. The hole is uphill, 390 yards long and, as the name suggests, the tee shot is through a portal of trees to a fairway that is about 150 yards or more away. The fairway slopes left to right and needs to be considered. The green is flanked by a series of bunkers on the left and has a false front to boot.

Number thirteen, *Defiance*, is an uphill par-three demanding all of your attention. It is 216 yards long and has a steeply faced bunker guarding most of the green's front, as well as two smaller ones at the right rear.

*Revenge*, the fourteenth hole, challenges you with a downhill, narrow fairway. It is 443 yards long with a lateral water hazard guarding the right side of the fairway. Approximately sixty yards in front of the green, and in the dead center of the fairway, is a large bunker, which should not affect anything, but you will see it and quake a bit. The green needs careful observation and study, since it has more break than any other green on the golf course. The 393 yard fifteenth, Dragon's Fire, is

aptly named, because it could cause you to get hot under your collar. The tee shot plays downhill over an arroyo and has to land on a fairway that slopes severely left to right. Next are a few large pines in the fairway that interfere with a shot to the green, which has a ridge suitable for tobogganing, running down the middle.

The sixteenth, *Audacity*, is a long par-four measuring 495 yards. The number two handicap hole on the card, it may easily be the hardest on the course. With a long drive along the right side, which actually is wider than it looks from the tee, you'll have a good angle to a green that is tucked into the forest at the left side of the fairway. Take your time selecting your club to get to the green. It is shallow and fast.

The seventeenth, *Dragon's Pearl*, is the last par-three, a slightly uphill 175-yarder to a green that is divided in two by a ridge. Stopping your ball on the proper tier will make your putt a lot easier.

The finishing hole, *Enlightenment*, is a par-five of 559 yards. To bolster the chance of getting on the green in two, the tee shot should be placed as close to the left-side bunker as possible. The other bunkers are all down the right side, with a single one just in front. Avoid them….they have steep faces.

THE TENTH, ONE OF ONLY THREE HOLES WHERE WATER COMES INTO PLAY

Since The Dragon opened for play in 2000, it has developed the intended reputation as the new gold standard in golf courses that present a challenge to even the most accomplished players. Unfortunately, the word most often used is not challenging but unfair.

As the game developed, golf courses evolved from playing on fields that had no special preparation to courses that had a lot of preparation. Along with that, the mindset also changed, more so in the United States than in Europe. Playing on a linksland course like Ballybunion, or Lahinch, I dare say no player would ever call it unfair when his ball, right in the middle of the fairway, mind you, came to rest in an awkward place, forcing the player to negotiate a sidehill lie in an otherwise level fairway. That's called "rub of the green."

If you need to have a level lie on every shot you walk up to in the fairway, or if, when the ball is a little above or below your feet, you don't take pride in being able to make the necessary adjustment, or if every time the ball breaks an inch just before it gets to the cup and then lips out, well, The Dragon is probably not for you.

On the other hand if you recognize that dealing with these quirky happenings is what golf is about and will result in an improvement to your game that can't be read in books, or bought through lessons, then you may have found a home.

Difficult courses are only difficult if you get yourself entangled in the designer's web. Appreciating the design of a golf course, the purpose of an obstruction and perhaps most important, choosing the appropriate tee leads to good golf.

It is, after all, a game that's played between your ears.

| HOLE | Dragon's Lookout | Deception | Simplicity | Faith | Hope | Charity | Dragon's Tail | Looking Glass | Perseverance | | PLAYERS | Dragon Lagoon | Teeth of The Dragon | Dragon's Gate | Defiance | Revenge | Dragon's Fire | Audacity | Dragon's Pearl | Enlightenment | | |
|---|---|---|---|---|---|---|---|---|---|---|---|---|---|---|---|---|---|---|---|---|---|---|
| Dragon 6 | 533 | 458 | 400 | 320 | 164 | 456 | 499 | 192 | 398 | 3420 | | 433 | 553 | 390 | 216 | 443 | 393 | 495 | 175 | 559 | 3657 | 7077 |
| Dragon 5 | 513 | 438 | 385 | 312 | 142 | 437 | 471 | 185 | 375 | 3258 | | 421 | 539 | 357 | 185 | 430 | 377 | 475 | 167 | 540 | 3491 | 6749 |
| Dragon 4 | 482 | 415 | 371 | 304 | 126 | 411 | 447 | 169 | 347 | 3072 | | 400 | 504 | 341 | 160 | 398 | 371 | 448 | 162 | 524 | 3308 | 6380 |
| Dragon 3 | 455 | 382 | 358 | 291 | 108 | 381 | 414 | 148 | 325 | 2862 | | 394 | 489 | 319 | 146 | 373 | 353 | 404 | 125 | 480 | 3083 | 5945 |
| Dragon 2 | 447 | 364 | 241 | 267 | 89 | 311 | 397 | 108 | 265 | 2489 | | 368 | 477 | 213 | 121 | 367 | 336 | 375 | 100 | 443 | 2800 | 5289 |
| Dragon 1 | 412 | 324 | 235 | 192 | 64 | 254 | 367 | 88 | 259 | 2195 | | 352 | 438 | 209 | 94 | 321 | 150 | 358 | 80 | 414 | 2416 | 4611 |
| Men's HDCP | 11 | 5 | 9 | 15 | 17 | 1 | 13 | 7 | 5 | | | 6 | 4 | 12 | 10 | 8 | 16 | 2 | 18 | 14 | | |
| | | | | | | | | | | | | | | | | | | | | | | |
| | | | | | | | | | | | | | | | | | | | | | | |
| | | | | | | | | | | | | | | | | | | | | | | |
| Women's HDCP | 7 | 3 | 11 | 13 | 17 | 1 | 9 | 15 | 5 | | | 6 | 10 | 8 | 12 | 4 | 14 | 2 | 18 | 16 | | |

Date: _____  Scorer: _____  Attest: _____  Tees Played: 6 5 1 3 2 1

MOHAWK VALLEY IS A SERENE AND PEACEFUL place. At an altitude of about forty-five hundred feet, it is surrounded on all sides by mountain peaks that protect this natural sanctuary against the outside world. There are seasons, but moderation seems to be the key. There is snow in the winter but not a lot, summer without excruciating heat, and fall is just about the best time of the year. Most of the time it's just plain pleasant, a few brooks gurgling away, flowers and grasses weaving in a light breeze, birds chirping with other animals looking on. A bit like Camelot, perhaps?

956 acres, a good portion of the Mohawk Valley, was acquired by Hugh White in 1979 with the intention of building an equestrian center. This turned out to be not such a good idea, and the White family changed direction and decided on a golf course with an adjoining real estate development. They would market this as a second-home lifestyle choice for

# Whitehawk Ranch Golf Club

*6,927 yards, par 71*

*Architect: Dick Bailey*

*Opened for play: 1995*

*Altitude: 4,516 feet*

*Head Professional: Doug Flynn*

*THE SECOND HOLE SEEN FROM ACROSS THE MANY PONDS*

active seniors, with many outdoor activities at their doorstep.

Dick Bailey was chosen to design and supervise the construction, even though this would be his first effort as a golf architect. He had been a developer, creating golf projects with the likes of Tom Weiskopf. It quickly became apparent to the Whites that running a golf course also was not what they had in mind, and through Bailey they were introduced to Jim Bartlett and Nick Hackstock, who are responsible for, among others, the Lahonton country club development in Truckee. The deal struck had Bartlett and Hackstock purchasing the golf course from the White family and running it as a separate entity, with Marcia White, Hugh's daughter, heading the housing

development. At the end of 2005, the development is sold out.

Practically every golf architect today, when asked to design a course, is also required to make it accessible to a wide variety of golfers. Excluding potential customers who can't carry a hundred-yard waste area, even though they want to, would not be prudent. What is needed is a course that has challenging back tees and forward tees that take the agony out of the game for the distance-challenged, with two tees in between. That's what Bailey accomplished. He designed a course that pleases all levels of the golfing population, which is undoubtedly the reason that Doug Flynn, Whitehawk Ranch's head professional, sends twenty thousand golfers around the course in a season. That's quite a fantastic number when you consider that there are only about a hundred yearly memberships and the season is only six months long. What is also extraordinary is that Whitehawk was named on a top-twenty list by *Golf Digest.*

The opening hole of a golf course requires special care by the designer. Primary consideration must be given to who will be playing the course and to what purpose. Recreational golfers and occasional players deserve a chance to begin a round on a positive note. At Tilden Park in Berkeley, California, the opening hole is a 411-yard par-four, an uphill monstrosity that

*NUMBER FIVE FAIRWAY FROM BEHIND THE GREEN*

*THE EIGHTH GREEN AT TOP AND THE FOURTEENTH GREEN BELOW*

demands a straight shot or controlled draw off the tee, to a usually soggy fairway, then a second to an elevated and bunkered green. It's not an ideal way to start a round.

The opening hole at Whitehawk, on the other hand, is a 396-yard par-four that has the right mix of elements for a good opener. It is a straight hole with a generous landing area in front of a very large bunker on the left. Anywhere short of the bunker will give you a relatively short iron to the green. The green has no bunkers and some mounding that will funnel the ball to the proper place. Number two is a little tougher in that there is water on the left, with the fairway curling in that direction. The tendency, of course, is to try to get close to the water, shaving off valuable yards. On a 412-yard hole, this bravery might be necessary to have a chance at par.

The greens for the most part are two-tiered and have gentle undulations with pleasing lines. None of the greens are bunkered behind, but most have mounding that will catch long shots, and in some cases can require awkward pitches back. The design produces "quadrants"—areas that are about twenty feet in diameter. Get the ball within that area and the putts will be straight, but outside that anything is possible.

Number three, the first par-three is 231 yards long. The

green has several plateaus, which makes for trouble if you end up on the wrong level. These opening holes have been in a meadow. The fourth, a transition hole, starts in the meadow but winds up in thick forest. It is a long par-four at 481 yards, slightly uphill and the number-one handicap hole. Like many holes on this layout, it will test your skill with the long irons or fairway woods on the second shot. The green is free of surrounding bunkers but is long and difficult to read.

Bunkers on this course are large. Sand must have been inexpensive in 1994. The sculpting is beautiful, with a variety of shapes only an artist could envision. But their shapes can and will produce predicaments not conducive to low scores. Mostly, though, they serve as targets, but they are targets to stay out of.

The next four holes have only one trait in common—they are in the trees. Five is straight, six is a dogleg and seven is the kind of beautiful par-three that just begs for a great shot. The eighth, a 543-yard par-five, stretches a long way downhill into the sunlight and then a long way to the green.

The ninth is the short par-four every course needs. At 310 yards, the green is reachable with an accurate drive, but be warned that there is water on the right. For those who respect the design, make sure you don't go too far off the tee, since

there is a rill crossing the fairway thirty yards in front of the green.

The Sulfur Creek defines the golf course, most notably beside the tenth and eighteenth fairways. There is a system of ponds, joined by rills that often determine club selection by where they run across the fairways. The reeds and grasses that grow in these small streams greatly enhance the look of the course. In 1996 there was a "hundred-year" storm that swelled the river to such a degree that it took out the eighteenth, and tenth holes. Craig Pearson, the course's greenkeeper, reclaimed the land, and with Bailey's input the two holes were rebuilt. To commemorate this effort, the little creek running across the ninth fairway will be known as Pearson Creek.

The tenth starts the back nine with a strong challenge. It's a very long hole at 464 yards, and it takes a good drive and a great long-iron approach to have a chance for a par. The mountain peak that appears in the California state flag is fashioned after Eureka Peak, which can be seen in the distance beyond the tenth green.

The eleventh hole is a pretty par-three of 202 yards, one

*OVERLEAF:*
*NUMBER NINE AT TWILIGHT*

*51*

*THE OPENING HOLE WITH EUREKA PEAK IN THE DISTANCE ABOVE,*
*AND THE LANDING AREA WITH THE GIANT BUNKER AT LEFT*

hundred and four yards shorter from the most forward tee, which is the only one of the four tee positions that does not go over water.

Twelve, thirteen and fourteen are all challenging par-fours more than 400 yards long. A small stream cuts across the fairway and beside the green on one, in front of the tee box on the next, and along the fairway on the last. It doesn't really come into play on any of them but adds a delightful visual treat. The next, the par-five fifteenth, is 536 yards long, has a fairway bunker, out of reach for all, to aim at off the tee. This first landing area is quite generous, as is the next one short of the green. There is a small bunker to the right front.

Number sixteen is 175 yards, a slightly downhill par-three.

From the tee, the green does not look very wide, and the bunker beside it seems enormous. Seventeen curves to the left along Sulfur Creek. It's a par-four 431 yards long. The area around the green is dangerous. But this is just a preamble to the finishing hole. The eighteenth is 558 yards long, a par-five with a fairway that becomes narrower and narrower the closer you get to a pair of large bunkers. The closer you are to the bunkers, the less a group of trees in the middle of the fairway will come into play. Then there is the matter of a brook running across the fairway just in front of the green. Other than that, it's a piece of cake….one that can often send you to the 19th hole for sustenance of the more liquid variety.

Word of mouth has worked very well for this gorgeous layout's success over the last ten years. Groups of golfers come from the San Francisco Bay area, stay in the cabins at The Lodge, and just enjoy. And now, no longer a well-kept secret, Whitehawk is ready for the world.

| Hole | Four Hawk | Three Hawk | Two Hawk | | | | Par | Handicap | | One Hawk | Hole | Four Hawk | Three Hawk | Two Hawk | | | | Par | Handicap | | One Hawk |
|---|---|---|---|---|---|---|---|---|---|---|---|---|---|---|---|---|---|---|---|---|---|
| 1 | 396 | 366 | 328 | | | | 4 | 9 | | 274 | 10 | 464 | 445 | 400 | | | | 4 | 2 | | 300 |
| 2 | 412 | 368 | 336 | | | | 4 | 3 | | 283 | 11 | 202/191 | 179/160 | 148/129 | | | | 3 | 16 | | 129/98 |
| 3 | 231 | 203 | 164 | | | | 3 | 11 | | 117 | 12 | 419 | 405 | 345 | | | | 4 | 14 | | 285 |
| 4 | 481 | 449 | 411 | | | | 4 | 1 | | 329 | 13 | 434 | 408 | 344 | | | | 4 | 8 | | 302 |
| 5 | 348 | 328 | 271 | | | | 4 | 17 | | 248 | 14 | 417 | 372 | 317 | | | | 4 | 12 | | 242 |
| 6 | 392 | 363 | 346 | | | | 4 | 5 | | 272 | 15 | 536 | 510 | 460 | | | | 5 | 10 | | 396 |
| 7 | 178 | 152 | 138 | | | | 3 | 15 | | 111 | 16 | 175 | 163 | 132 | | | | 3 | 18 | | 117/98 |
| 8 | 543 | 519 | 451 | | | | 5 | 7 | | 412 | 17 | 431 | 411 | 379 | | | | 4 | 4 | | 319 |
| 9 | 310 | 276 | 267 | | | | 4 | 13 | | 238 | 18 | 558 | 528 | 486 | | | | 5 | 6 | | 442 |
| Out | 3291 | 3024 | 2712 | | | | 35 | | | 2284 | In | 3636 | 3421 | 3011 | | | | 36 | | | 2532 |
| | | | | | | | | | | | Total | 6927 | 6445 | 5723 | | | | 71 | | | 4816 |

Scorer_____

Handicap

Attest_____ Date_____

Net

WHITEHAWK RANCH G.C.

BEGINNING BACK IN THE 1920s, LOGGING PINE and fir was the prime industry in the Truckee area, keeping two sawmills operating. Then, in 1970, the Tahoe Donner Association was formed. The first home was built in 1972, and now there are more than six thousand, most of them second homes for owners from Sacramento and the Bay Area.

The golf course was planned as a feature that would attract people to the area. It worked then, and that same business plan works today. The Tahoe Donner Golf Course was designed by Bob Williams and opened for play in 1976. The original design was a good one then, narrow fairways and greens that called for a good understanding of strategy and a deft touch. When the association thought it needed to update the course it turned to Carey Bickler. He did not redesign the layout, but he made it correspond to the distances new equipment was allowing golfers to

# *Tahoe Donner Golf Course*

*6,931 yards, par 72*

*Architect: Bob Williams*

*Opened for play: 1976*

*Altitude: 6,501 feet*

*Director of Golf: Bill Winfield*

achieve. To appeal to a wider audience, new forward tee boxes were added and a general facelift was included. It didn't look all that bad before, but now it's simply great.

Construction began on the new clubhouse, called The Lodge, in the summer of 2004, and the grand opening was in September 2005. The Lodge, which blends seamlessly into the landscape, provides meeting facilities, a pub, an elegant banquet room and an American Bistro style dining room for Tahoe Donner's members and visitors. It also houses the golf shop and offices for the golf staff.

Right below the clubhouse is a putting area that has some of the features of greens on the course, not nearly as tough but good enough to get you comfortable with your stroke. A chipping area, with a flag to shoot for, is twenty steps to the right, and one of the most beautiful driving ranges you'll ever see is a few hundred yards away....it's well worth the trip, especially if you want to get prepared for the opening hole..

Since this is a residential area, the golf course is bordered by houses that for the most part are set back far enough that they don't interfere with play. Just once in a while are there some homes that intrude on the natural look.

This is a fun golf course to play. There is the allegation that

*THE NINTH FAIRWAY FROM THE TEE ABOVE, AND
A MAJOR OBSTACLE IN THE NINTH FAIRWAY AT RIGHT*

golfers have to walk the course in single file because of its width. It isn't quite that narrow, since there are only four or five holes that make you hit your shots more accurately than you are used to. But that's good, isn't it?

The first is the number-one handicap hole, a 459-yard par-four, that by rights all first-time players ought to get to play twice. It is very narrow, the fairway slanting down from right to left with rough on both sides blending quite quickly into wilderness. About 150 yards from the green is a drainage ditch,

*THE SIXTH HOLE*

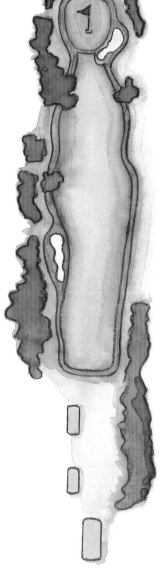

dry most of the time but a hard place to escape, although it's out of reach from the tee for most players. From this distance, the green is a mere sliver sitting a little above the fairway. There is a bunker on the left side and a few small trees on the right that guard the two-tiered green. This, your first chance to challenge the course's greens, is a moment to savor, especially if you avoid a three-putt.

Trees standing outside of the tree line on the right, a few yards into the groomed fairway, are a very nice but sinister design detail. Though not visible from the tee, once you get closer they can become an obstruction as solid as a wall.

The second hole is a 513-yard par-five, the narrow fairway rising to a plateau about 250 yards away, then for the last eighty yards dropping about 20 feet down to the green. The green is not too wide and fairly deep, but still there is a danger of running off the back.

As I'm walking the course, it occurs to me that golfers riding in carts miss a lot of the natural beauty as it unfolds around you, the placement of obstacles that mostly are not obvious from the side in a speeding cart, and just plain being with yourself and the course.

The third is a fairly long par-four at 439 yards. With a

*THE NEW CLUBHOUSE OPENED SEPTEMBER 2005*

good drive you might have a middle iron left to the green. Contradicting common configuration, the fairway gets wider as you get closer to the green. The green is about forty-five yards deep and has undulations on top of undulations. Getting your approach shot close to the hole would be a good thing.

The fourth, the first par-three, is about two hundred yards to a green that is about ten or fifteen feet above the teeing ground, and is protected by three bunkers, one of which wraps around half the front. The green rises steadily to the back, making a putt coming back down a heart-pounder.

Number five is a par-four of only 377 yards with a rather wide fairway and not much trouble around the green. This will just get you warmed up for the sixth, the feature hole, a par-

EIGHTEEN LOOKING BACK UP THE SLOPE, ABOVE
AND FROM THE TEE AT RIGHT

NUMBER TWO GREEN ABOVE TOP, THE DOGLEG AT THIRTEEN ABOVE
AND THE FIRST HOLE LOOKING BACK TO THE CLUBHOUSE AT RIGHT

four of 357 yards. Starting out, the fairway has a slight rise, presenting a horizon of woods on the right and a thirty-yard-long bunker on the left, along with a huge tree smack dab in the middle 180 yards from the tee. There are two options: get past the tree on the right or get past it on the left. Either is good and sets up a second shot to a green that is trapped on the right, surrounded by tall pine trees and quite a bit below your feet. About fifty yards short of the green are two large pines with the fairway running between them that can make this shot a bit like kicking a field goal.

Number seven, a par-three of medium length at 163 yards that was recently refurbished, will usually play downwind. This beautiful setting deserves, no, demands a good shot. The green is difficult to read, given the many undulations, putting emphasis on club selection and execution to get close. The bunker on the left side has a steep face, and the opening to the green is mounded. The eighth hole is a downhill, dogleg-right par-four of 470 yards. From the tee there is an outcropping that juts into the fairway, fifteen or twenty yards, reducing it to half its width. Getting past this obstacle and cutting off as much of the corner as possible makes the shot to the green, which has to carry a trench, almost routine….almost.

The 550-yard ninth also was given a coat of new grass and new irrigation, but the same long look was kept. It will take even big hitters two good shots to get to the green in regulation. There are some bunkers, a small one on the left and an eighty-foot sculpted monster on the right, to show you where and how far you must hit your drive. The green is well bunkered, as is the left fairway short of the green.

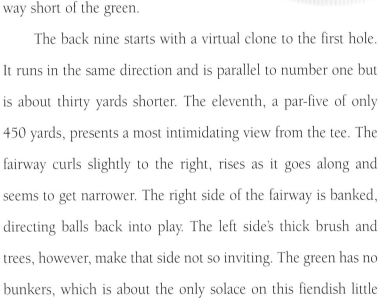

The back nine starts with a virtual clone to the first hole. It runs in the same direction and is parallel to number one but is about thirty yards shorter. The eleventh, a par-five of only 450 yards, presents a most intimidating view from the tee. The fairway curls slightly to the right, rises as it goes along and seems to get narrower. The right side of the fairway is banked, directing balls back into play. The left side's thick brush and trees, however, make that side not so inviting. The green has no bunkers, which is about the only solace on this fiendish little devil of a hole.

The twelfth is a par-three of 200 yards, with the flat, thirty-five-yard deep green rising toward the back. It is probably the

THE SEVENTH IN ITS NEW GLORY, A 163-YARD PAR-THREE

easiest green on the course to read. The thirteenth is a par-four of only 320 yards that doglegs severely to the left. It's only a good five-iron to the mounded turn, then a six- or seven-iron to get to the large green that, uncharacteristically, is easily read.

Number fourteen, a par-four of 391 yards, plays longer than that. There's a trench in the landing area that needs to be carried and another that requires you to play short. There are some bunkers beyond the second trench that aren't really in play. The green, large and intimidating, returns to the tough, undulating mode. The fifteenth, a par-five that is 519 yards long, has drainage ditches running diagonally across the fairway twice, neither of which should be in play. The green sets up nicely, with bunkers left and right but a fairly wide opening to the putting surface. This hole decides many a competition.

Sixteenth is the number-two handicap hole, a 453-yard par-four. With a very slight rise in combination with a relatively narrow fairway this hole has reason to be so high on the handicap pole. Seventeen is a lengthy par three at 226 yards, mostly downhill to a large, undulating, bunkered green that is very hard to hit and once on even harder to read. The finishing hole is 422 yards long, starting severely downhill. The tee shot should reach a relatively flat area that cannot be seen from the

tee; in fact there is a periscope to let you ascertain that the group in front has left. The shot to the green is wonderful. Just in front is a brook that has plenty of tall grasses and balloons out into a little pond. The green is heavily bunkered and again can be hard to read.

Competitions and tournament play are the lifeblood of golf, so it is good to see that there are several active groups at Tahoe Donner. There is a Men's Club that meets every Wednesday at high noon and a Woman's Club, as well as a Nine-hole club for women, both of which meet every Tuesday morning. The inaugural year for the Mark Wellman Celebrity Golf Challenge, a fund-raising event that will benefit disabled athletes, was 2005. Many celebrities as well as Olympians came to Truckee to participate, which made it a very successful event at a very successful golf facility.

| HOLE | | 1 | 2 | 3 | 4 | 5 | 6 | 7 | 8 | 9 | OUT | I | 10 | 11 | 12 | 13 | 14 | 15 | 16 | 17 | 18 | IN | TOT | HCP | NET |
|---|---|---|---|---|---|---|---|---|---|---|---|---|---|---|---|---|---|---|---|---|---|---|---|---|---|
| Blue | 73.5/132 | 459 | 513 | 445 | 201 | 377 | 357 | 163 | 469 | 581 | 3565 | N | 423 | 449 | 200 | 320 | 391 | 519 | 453 | 226 | 422 | 3403 | 6968 | | |
| White | 72.3/129 | 438 | 483 | 435 | 192 | 369 | 349 | 146 | 451 | 544 | 3407 | I | 390 | 441 | 152 | 310 | 369 | 503 | 442 | 203 | 398 | 3208 | 6615 | | |
| Handicap | | 1 | 9 | 5 | 11 | 17 | 13 | 15 | 3 | 7 | | T | 4 | 6 | 12 | 18 | 14 | 8 | 2 | 16 | 10 | | | | |
| Men's Par | | 4 | 5 | 4 | 3 | 4 | 4 | 3 | 4 | 5 | 36 | I A L | 4 | 5 | 3 | 4 | 4 | 5 | 4 | 3 | 4 | 36 | 72 | | |
| | | | | | | | | | | | | | | | | | | | | | | | | | |
| | | | | | | | | | | | | | | | | | | | | | | | | | |
| | | | | | | | | | | | | | | | | | | | | | | | | | |
| | | | | | | | | | | | | | | | | | | | | | | | | | |
| Ladies' Par | | 5 | 5 | 4 | 3 | 4 | 4 | 3 | 4 | 5 | 37 | | 4 | 5 | 3 | 4 | 4 | 5 | 4 | 3 | 4 | 36 | 73 | | |
| Handicap | | 6 | 2 | 8 | 16 | 12 | 14 | 18 | 10 | 4 | | | 7 | 1 | 17 | 15 | 9 | 5 | 11 | 13 | 3 | | | | |
| Red | 72.7/137 | 366 | 422 | 351 | 147 | 308 | 340 | 132 | 336 | 453 | 2855 | | 351 | 430 | 130 | 301 | 352 | 491 | 356 | 182 | 343 | 2936 | 5791 | | |
| Target Times | | :15 | :32 | :47 | :59 | 1:13 | 1:27 | 1:37 | 1:51 | 2:09 | | | 2:23 | 2:39 | 2:51 | 3:05 | 3:18 | 3:35 | 3:49 | 4:01 | 4:15 | | | | |
| Scorer: | | | | | | | © Golf ScoreCards 06/2005 1-800-236-7267 | | | | | Attest: | | | | | | | | | | Date: | | | |

# Coyote Moon Golf Course

*7,177 yards, par 72*

*Architect: Homer Flint & Brad Bell*

*Opened for play: 2000*

*Altitude: 6,284 feet*

*Head Professional: Dirk Skillicorn*

THE MARK OF AN OUTSTANDING GOLF COURSE is that it demands an outstanding performance. What a player needs to demonstrate on his way to an outstanding round is the ability to hit long, straight shots, accurate in distance as well as direction, to use all clubs in the bag and, if that weren't enough, to make the ball turn left or right as needed. Reading the greens and judging the speed, whether on level or severely sloping terrain, makes this part of the game equally important. Coyote Moon serves up a dish that contains all these ingredients in abundance. It also offers thoughtful forward tee locations for golfers with less distance off the tee.

The scenic wonder that is the High Sierra is present at every turn. The air is clean, it hardly ever rains, and during the summer the temperature is mostly in the eighties. Should you be fortunate enough to be on the course late in the day with sunlight filtering

THE EARLY MORNING SUNLIGHT STREAMS ACROSS THE THIRTEENTH GREEN through the trees, you will see colors unknown to most. The season is cut short by extreme winter conditions, but the course is in wonderful condition when it opens in April and remains that way all year, thanks to Dirk Skillicorn and his dedicated staff. Starting in 2007, Dirk will move over to Gray's Crossing, and Shane Jones will take over the helm at Coyote Moon.

Before development began in earnest, this was primarily a logging area. Homer Flint did the first routing plan on just such a logging tract, which Brad Bell refined and implemented in 1995. Flint has a distinguished record as a golf architect and is responsible for Plumas Pines and Northstar, two other courses in the Sierra Nevada. The routing plan is critical to the final product, akin to the foundation of a house. A weak foundation eventually will cause the structure to collapse. A sound routing plan gives that sound foundation to a course.

Brad Bell is a former PGA Tour player from Sacramento, a UCLA graduate with a degree in economics, and a two-time All-American. He spent two years on the European Tour, then played on the Ben Hogan Tour and finally qualified for the big show. He battled a hand injury for several years before he left competitive golf and pursued golf architecture. He became a designer for Steele Enterprises, a construction company

NUMBER TWELVE FAIRWAY ABOVE, AND A CLOSEUP OF THE GREEN AT RIGHT

involved in building golf courses. Besides Coyote Moon, Bell designed Teal Bend and Turkey Creek, both golf courses in Sacramento, as well as Empire Ranch Club in Folsom. He has built a reputation for creating courses that easily blend into the landscape and in fact enhance the existing natural beauty, which is no mean feat in the High Sierra.

Coyote Moon is now owned and operated by East West Partners, who are also responsible for Old Greenwood and the soon-to-open Gray's Crossing, all in Truckee. It should be noted that Coyote Moon Golf Course is the only course in this book that does not have residences lining the fairways. It is a golf

course, pure and simple. Clubs can be rented and lessons taken, and there is a restaurant that will serve a good lunch and a cold beer over which to ponder your round. But as soon as the last golfer leaves, the lights go out, and the golf course awaits the next sunrise.

During the planning and construction phases, the working title for the golf course was "Truckee Falls" but was changed to Coyote Moon for the opening. The name was deemed inappropriate by the management company running the day-to-day operation and was changed to "Pine Ridge Golf." I'm not sure how important the name of a golf course is, but the locals objected to the change and convinced management to revert to Coyote Moon. Hopefully this is the final christening.

Although there probably would have been the acreage, there is no formal driving range. There is a more-than-adequate putting and chipping area and a rubber mat, just large enough for an on-deck foursome to hit a few balls into a net twenty feet away. Driving ranges are after all a modern phenomenon; some of the great courses, such as Cypress Point, Pine Valley, Merion, Pebble Beach, Seminole and Augusta National all were built without practice tees. The solution Coyote Moon gives the combatants is a very good one, though. It allows them to take a full

swing and feel and hear how the clubhead meets the ball. Because they can't see the ball fly through the air, adjustments and new ideas just before the round are rightfully discouraged.

From the tee the entire first hole can be seen in all its robust glory. It very plainly displays the features you'll see over and over again on this magnificent course. But don't let the scenery distract you. This first hole is a relatively narrow uphill, 519-yard par-five. Reaching the green in two shots is only possible for the longest hitters. For the rest, a tee shot up the left side and an approach to the right will avoid all the bunkering on the left, setting up the third shot to the green. The green has two plateaus separated by a ridge that creates about a two foot height difference and is guarded by two sizable bunkers in front, one about a hundred yards in front of the green and one to the side. Putting skills will be tested on this and the greens to come, which bears out the sensibility of having such a large practice putting facility.

The second is a fairly long par-four at 447 yards, requiring two solid shots to get to the green and testing your distance control with the fairway woods or long irons. A long bunker on the left side about one hundred yards short of the green seldom comes into play, but it can be your aiming point off the tee.

*THE GIGANTIC BOULDER AT THE SEVENTH GREEN*

LOOKING BACK TO THE FAIRWAY ON NUMBER ELEVEN ABOVE,
AND THE FIFTEENTH GREEN AND FAIRWAY AT RIGHT

The third hole, the first par-three, is about two hundred yards long, depending on the hole location. A favoring wind often takes the pressure off, but should the green be missed short, there is mounding that will misdirect your ball to any number of places. There is a peanut-shaped bunker short and left. The green itself is about one hundred feet deep and has the usual Coyote Moon undulations.

The fourth hole's landing area slants from left to right and favors a strong draw into the hill and around the bend. This is a very demanding hole of about 440 yards. Number five, a 404-yard par-four, has a forced carry of almost two hundred yards from the tee to the beginning of the fairway, which then rises sharply to a plateau. The setting for the green is nothing if not spectacular, with a clover leaf bunker cutting into the green on the right. The sixth is a 396 yard long par-four and asks the player for a draw off the tee for the best strategic position into the green. The bunker on the right side 190 yards out should be carried to a fairway that bulges out behind the trap.

Number seven is a par-five 527 yards long and can be reached in two shots. The drive first has to carry an irrigation lake, then stay left of a bunker. The fairway starts out quite wide but narrows the farther your ball travels. The green is tightly bunkered and is about one hundred feet deep.

The front edge of the eighth green is only about one hundred and fifty yards from the tee, the back about forty yards farther. It's the shortest hole on the golf course, the number 17 handicap, but can be tricky if the pin is placed behind the solitary bunker.

Numbers nine, ten and eleven are very long and narrow par-fours measuring 434, 433 and 468 yards, respectively. Eleven has a most interesting tee shot that should be aimed at a fairway trap on the left side with a slight fade. Twelve is a gorgeous uphill par-five, 519 yards long, that should be savored. The green is surrounded by large boulders, a lone bunker in front and two larger ones behind the green.

Number thirteen, Coyote Moon's feature hole, is probably the most interesting hole on the course, due to an extreme difference in altitude—about ninety feet—from tee to green. It measures 248 yards from the tee, but we're not told how this is measured. The first time you hit a ball here, you will watch the

*THE SPECTACULAR MOUNTAIN BACKGROUND AT THE FIFTH GREEN*

*NUMBER THIRTEEN, A 227-YARD PAR-THREE*

trajectory with amazement. Very few players use enough club their first time, thus landing in Trout Creek and then using the drop area for the third shot. The green is narrow and long and is positioned at a forty-five degree angle to the shot. One bunker in front and one behind the green round out this witch's brew of trouble.

The fourteenth hole is a par-four of less than three hundred yards. The fairway starts approximately one hundred yards from the tee and parallels Trout Creek, which runs its entire length. The green, which also runs parallel to the fairway but is on the other side of the creek, is shaped a bit like a dachshund, long and not too wide. A pine tree toward the end and in the middle of the fairway needs to be avoided but can be used as a target. This hole, as in most short par-fours, can be played in any number of ways, but there is a need for accuracy. The green offers many interesting hole locations, and the undulations create challenging putts.

The fifteenth requires brawn. It is 601 yards long and demands three solid shots to navigate. The back tee, testament to its length and the number of people using it, is so small that a foursome having a picnic would just barely fit. The fairway gets quite narrow and ends abruptly about one hundred and

GOLF COURSES OF THE HIGH SIERRA

thirty yards from the green. A river bed and then a sheer man-made rock wall loom in your path. Beyond this the fairway continues to a green that has two levels and a front that requires your shot to carry onto the putting surface. It's a terrifying golf hole but an extremely satisfying one if you master it.

Number sixteen is a very well-designed par-three hole of 212 yards, quite often playing straight into the prevailing wind. The green is tucked between a lake and a fairly steep slope leading up to the parking lot, which is not in view. Fronting the green is a retaining wall made of boulders that signals a stern warning not to be short.

There are two visual errors on this otherwise flawless course. One is the cart paths often cutting in front of tees and across fairways. The other is the maintenance building that seems to be forever in one's line of sight. This is especially so on the sixteenth, which could be one of the best-looking holes on the course but whose beauty is marred by this ugly building behind it that easily could have been put elsewhere.

The two finishing par-fours have a lot of character, presenting different challenges. Both deserve thought. Seventeen is 472 yards long, with the shortest route demanding a 254-yard carry over a lake, less if you stay to the left of the lake, then a 180-yard shot to the green, which has a bunker at the rear. If possible, your approach should come in softly. Eighteen is quite different. At 341 yards it is the second shortest par-four on the course, another strategic gem. With a good tee shot there is probably only a short iron left to the green, which will be a handful to putt if your ball winds up outside the comfort zone.

These two holes combine to provide a great finish on a beautiful mountain course that stretches your skills to the limit. Homer Flint's routing plan has proven to be a good one, and it can only be hoped that he has given his nod of approval to the finished product. We certainly have.

| HOLE | BLACK | BLUE | WHITE | HANDICAP | | | | | | HANDICAP | GOLD |
|---|---|---|---|---|---|---|---|---|---|---|---|
| 1 | 561 | 519 | 469 | 9 | | | 5 | | | 13 | 392 |
| 2 | 447 | 404 | 382 | 5 | | | 4 | | | 7 | 317 |
| 3 | 207 | 186 | 156 | 15 | | | 3 | | | 15 | 124 |
| 4 | 441 | 426 | 408 | 1 | | | 4 | | | 1 | 335 |
| 5 | 404 | 389 | 369 | 3 | | | 4 | | | 3 | 301 |
| 6 | 396 | 377 | 354 | 13 | | | 4 | | | 9 | 278 |
| 7 | 527 | 507 | 478 | 11 | | | 5 | | | 11 | 377 |
| 8 | 173 | 158 | 127 | 17 | | | 3 | | | 17 | 107 |
| 9 | 434 | 406 | 377 | 7 | | | 4 | | | 5 | 328 |
| OUT | 3590 | 3372 | 3120 | | | | 36 | | | | 2559 |
| 10 | 433 | 408 | 389 | 6 | | | 4 | | | 4 | 306 |
| 11 | 468 | 436 | 407 | 10 | | | 4 | | | 18 | 339 |
| 12 | 519 | 492 | 458 | 14 | | | 5 | | | 10 | 387 |
| 13 | 227 | 206 | 187 | 8 | | | 3 | | | 16 | 108 |
| 14 | 314 | 294 | 243 | 18 | | | 4 | | | 12 | 211 |
| 15 | 601 | 557 | 541 | 4 | | | 5 | | | 2 | 461 |
| 16 | 212 | 183 | 161 | 12 | | | 3 | | | 6 | 112 |
| 17 | 472 | 454 | 412 | 2 | | | 4 | | | 8 | 312 |
| 18 | 341 | 312 | 295 | 16 | | | 4 | | | 14 | 227 |
| IN | 3587 | 3332 | 3091 | | | | 36 | | | | 2463 |
| TOT | 7177 | 6704 | 6211 | | | | 72 | | | | 5022 |
| HANDICAP | | | | | | | | | | | |
| NET SCORE | | | | | | | | | | | |
| DATE | | | SCORER | | | | ATTEST | | | | |

# Old Greenwood

*7,518 yards, par 72*

*Architect: Jack Nicklaus*

*Opened for play: 2004*

*Altitude: 6,004 feet*

*Director of Golf: Bob Hickam*

"OLD" CALEB GREENWOOD WAS A MOUNTAIN man who led hundreds of immigrants across the Sierra Nevada to California by what came to be known as the Emigrant Trail. The first among those to make the journey, in 1844, with Caleb Greenwood as their scout, was a group of fifty souls known as the Stephens-Townsend-Murphy party. At that time "Old" Caleb was in his eighties. A portion of that trail cuts across the Old Greenwood property; hence it seemed appropriate to immortalize him by naming this lofty development after him.

Caleb Greenwood may have given his name and his inspiration to the development, but it took East West Partners to use their imaginations and talents to bring a golf course to life, a course that in the first few months after opening for play was voted among the best ten new public access courses by *Golf Magazine.*

East West Partners is a resort development con-

NUMBER EIGHTEEN, AS SEEN FROM THE CLUBHOUSE PATIO

*VARIOUS MARKERS, STYLISHLY DESIGNED*

cern that has many successful efforts to its credit. Beaver Creek Resort in Colorado is one of their best. They are very active in Truckee, operating Coyote Moon Golf Course and expanding their portfolio with Gray's Crossing, which will open in 2007. This course will be designed by Peter Jacobsen and Jim Hardy, whose list of designs includes The Oregon Golf Club, Cypress Ridge Golf Course and Blackhorse Golf Club. Gray's Crossing will be a community located just north of Old Greenwood and will be designed with a small town feel. It is named after another historic Truckee personality, a sawmill operator, who built one of the first bridges across the Truckee River.

Bob Hickam is director of golf at Old Greenwood. He is somewhat of an expert at opening great golf courses. He was involved in opening The Links at Spanish Bay for the Pebble Beach Company on the Monterey Peninsula, Tehama in Carmel for Clint Eastwood, and now Old Greenwood. He has surrounded himself with an able and competent staff. Shane Jones was his head professional until the end of the 2005 season, when he moved over to Coyote Moon Golf Course to work with Dirk Skillicorn who will oversee the opening of Gray's Crossing starting in 2007. Joel Blaker is director of agronomy, which doesn't mean he can make the grass grow at will, but he can, and does, keep this course in beautiful condition.

In addition to the golf course at Old Greenwood, there is a golf academy, a driving range, a tennis and fitness center, a swimming complex and a small conference center. This is in addition to all that the Truckee area already is famous for: downhill and cross-country skiing, water sports, the trout creeks and the hiking trails....not to mention the ballooning and soaring from the glider port just south of the property. All Old Greenwood needs is a supermarket and you would never have to leave. Perhaps Safeway delivers? There are homes under construction everywhere, but Old Greenwood's master plan calls for setbacks that allow homes to exist close to the fairway without interfering with the visual integrity of the golf course. Eventually there will be about three hundred residences on this six-hundred acre development.

*THE THIRD HOLE, A 196-YARD PAR-THREE*

*THE NATIVE GRASSES CAN BE A PROBLEM ON THE SIXTH*

The original offering consisted of ninety-nine properties. It was decided that to memorialize these lucky buyers, who knew a good thing when they saw one, was to hold a yearly commemorative tournament each September. Called "The Founder's Cup," this tournament is only open to those ninety-nine original owners, now and in the years to come. The first one was held in 2003, which Bob Yoder won. It was held at Coyote Moon Golf Course, because the Old Greenwood golf course was not yet opened for play.

Long gone are the days when rabbit holes along the route from the Firth of Forth beach to the town of St. Andrews in Scotland determined a golf course. Today the process is a slightly more complex one. So when it came time to select a firm to design their golf course, the decision-makers at East West Partners had an easy time. Their short and long lists had only one name: Nicklaus.

Jack Nicklaus has brought much to the game since he first addressed a golf ball more than half a century ago. He won eighty-three tournaments, including twenty major championships, over the span of forty-two years, culminating in his official retirement from competitive golf at St. Andrews in 2005.

Early in his playing career, he quietly involved himself in

golf course design. In an early collaboration with Pete Dye, he put his mark on courses like Harbor Town Golf Links on Hilton Head Island and John's Island in Vero Beach. After he launched his own firm, he collaborated with Desmond Muirhead on two courses in Mason, Ohio, the Grizzly and the Bruin courses at the Jack Nicklaus Sports Center at Kings Island. He also teamed with Muirhead in 1974 to design the Muirfield Village Golf Club in Dublin, Ohio, which for many has become Jack's club. Among his other works are Shoal Creek in Alabama, Grand Cypress and Loxahatchee in Florida, Valhalla in Kentucky and Glen Abbey in Ontario, Canada. His firm, Nicklaus Design, has built more than two hundred and fifty courses, about two hundred of them with his personal involvement and some thirty-five ranked in the top one hundred on various lists.

Almost one third of the courses created by Nicklaus Design have been selected as venues for PGA Tour events or amateur championships. He is joined by his four sons and a son-in-law, as well as a dedicated staff, to carve his legacy in turf by building golf courses that will pass the test of time. Says Nicklaus: "Designing a golf course is my total expression. My golf game can only go on so long, but what I have learned can be put into a piece of ground, and that will last beyond me."

*NUMBER FIVE GREEN*

There now are many golf courses around the world that have been given the special designation of a "Jack Nicklaus Signature Course," which signifies Nicklaus' personal attention and involvement in every aspect of the course's design and development, while also utilizing the special design and field talents of Jim Lipe and Chris Rule.

One of these is Old Greenwood, and as part of that

*OVERLEAF:*
*NUMBER SIX, A COMPLEX PAR-FIVE WITH MANY CHALLENGES*

*THE DOWNHILL OPENING HOLE CURVES GENTYLY TO THE RIGHT*

personal involvement, Jack attended the opening of the golf course on August 30, 2004. Invited guests were able to watch the threesome of Jack Nicklaus, Jack Nicklaus II and Peter Jacobsen officially open the course and on the following day, with the tees and flags left in the same positions, participate in The Old Greenwood Open Pro-Am.

This golf course is a Nicklaus design that really is user-friendly. The Kentucky bluegrass fairways are generous. The rough is maintained at a forgiving length, and the bent grass greens in general are not overly undulating, although they are laid out in plateaus, which makes it important to get on the proper level with the approach. Nicklaus says he designs his courses with the average player in mind, then installs back tees to accommodate longer hitters. Quite a few of the greens are situated at an angle to the approach shot and are tilted obliquely, rather than front to back.

The front nine holes form a tight loop, finishing back at the clubhouse, and the back nine make one giant oval, with housing inside this loop. Even though the course is only two years old, it appears to have been here forever.

The first tee is a way from the clubhouse, allowing the first tee shot to be struck in relative obscurity. To the left of the first tee is a very generous practice layout, with a driving range that has player access from both ends, a putting and a chipping area. The starter will greet you there, tell you about the course conditions, help you decide which of the four tees is appropriate, and set down the cart path rules. Those rules are easy, since there is only one—stay on the cart path.

Once on the tee of this 462 yard par-four, there is nothing intimidating as you look down the green carpet of the fairway. It turns gently from left to right, and most of us have that shot. The lone danger might be a straight shot along the left side that is executed a bit too well, the ball going through the fairway into the rough or behind the trees skirting the fairway that block the shot to the green. The green is guarded by a bunker on the right. The putting surface has two levels and some gentle undulations, and there is room to be short and run the ball onto the putting surface.

The second measures six hundred and thirty-one yards, the longest hole on the course, and understandably, is the number one handicap hole. Like the first, it turns gently to the right, but a straight and long tee shot will not even get you to the turn. The next shot requires a slight fade and should be directed to the right side to gain the best access to the green, which

*THE FIFTEENTH, A 221-YARD PAR-THREE*

is angled to the fairway. Aiming down the right side also will keep you clear of a series of six nasty bunkers that are not at all inviting. On your third, you would do well to take dead aim at the pin, because the green has some severe swells. It is much too early in the round to lose confidence in your putting.

Number three is a 196-yard par-three with a green that sets up diagonally to the tee shot. On the right is a series of bunkers that are in line from each of the four tee boxes and hopefully will focus your effort. A small pot bunker is behind the green and should not come into play. Before getting to the sand, though, there is a sea of grass to cross. The green is peanut-shaped and is relatively easy to read.

The fourth hole is a par-four of 383 yards. The sides of the fairway weave in and out, making an already slim target appear even smaller. The second shot with a short to medium iron will be to a narrow green fronted by three small bunkers. There are openings between them, but none wide enough to attempt running the ball onto the green.

Number five is the second-longest par-four at 484 grueling yards. To offset the length, at least to some extent, there is a fairly wide fairway. The green is guarded by a bunker on the left side, with a smaller pot bunker toward the back. A good long

iron to the green would be easiest if struck from the right side of the fairway, where, as you can imagine, you'll also find a fairway bunker. The green has three levels and was shaped in a most interesting way. It's a great hole on which to get warmed up for the next hole.

Even though Nicklaus claims that this "Signature" golf course does not have a "signature hole," the par-five, 578-yard sixth has all the ingredients to be just that. It is dramatic in all its dimensions, with water along the left side, native grasses that could hide buffalo and the potential for heroic shots….and it's also just plain pretty. For the long hitters there is no choice. You have to attempt to reach the green in two. A long tee shot that avoids the water and a long shot over the lake will make this work. For everyone else, take three shots and follow the curve of the lake around to the green, which is protected by two small bunkers and presents its own challenges.

The seventh is a par-three, 187 yards long, that resembles the famous Redan hole on the original course in North Berwick, Scotland. This shot is mostly over water to a two-tiered green.

Number eight is 357 yards long, a dogleg par-four that has bunkers in all the appropriate places. Unless your ball carries 260 yards in the air, you should not attempt hugging the right

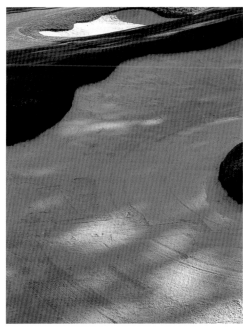

*NATIVE GRASSES, WATER OR SAND, SOMETIMES
ALL THREE, THESE ARE SOME OF THE
OBSTACLES TO CHALLENGE YOUR GAME*

*NUMBER SEVENTEEN*

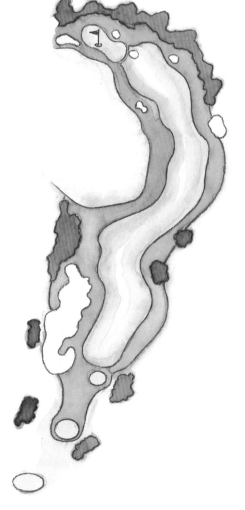

side. Staying close to those bunkers on their left side will leave you with just a wedge to the green, which is about thirty feet wide and one hundred feet deep, with two bunkers on the right side. Staying with the Scottish theme of the previous hole, Mr. Nicklaus also placed a little pot bunker right in the middle of the fairway about seventy yards from the green. Should this be in play for you, there is a strategic faux pas.

Fairway bunkers on the course are plentiful and are usually penal, especially if your ball ends up close to the lip. They are designed a bit like a roach motel—easy to get in but not so easy to get out. Not that the ball can't be advanced, but it often happens that if a crisp five-iron is needed to get to the pin, you may need an eight-iron to clear the lip. In some cases, on the eighteenth, for example, the bunkers are about six feet deep in front and not as deep behind the green. On this course the bunkers do what they were meant to accomplish. They are placed so that the player knows where not to go. And, should you go wrong, they exact a penalty. The same goes for greenside bunkers. Occasionally, with today's good equipment and improved technique, players find it beneficial to have a bunker stop their ball, but on this course that may not always be the right decision.

The ninth hole is an uphill 452 yard par-four. On the right side of the fairway are two pines that could very well interfere with your shot to the green, making anywhere left of those trees the preferred line. From that side, the green is more accessible as well. There are a few smallish bunkers on the right side of the green, which curls behind them. A pin placement behind these pot bunkers might be called sadistic.

Number ten has some of the same features we saw at the sixth. It is a par-five, 600 yards long, with water on the left from tee to green. The fairway curves to the left, with the third shot to the green quite possibly having to go over the lake in order to reach the putting surface. The few small bunkers on the hole are mainly for direction and decoration.

The eleventh is a treacherous short par-four of 345 yards. This hole will test your restraint. Those who hit the ball a long way have a chance of showing their bravado by going for the green off the tee. A more conservative approach is to aim for the fat of the fairway just past the bunker's left side, then try to get it close with a short iron.

Number twelve is a 551-yard par-five and a most scenic hole. Trees line the fairway, the undulations producing unimaginable shades of green. At about one hundred and twenty yards from the green, the fairway is forced to curve around a large trap resembling a bear's paw. It then sweeps right to the green, which is guarded by a bunker at the front left and a small one at the rear. During the opening round, Nicklaus smashed a four-wood about 240 yards, landing on the green and winding up inches from the flag for an eagle.

In case you've been holding back on your driver, the thirteenth is the hole where "getting all of it" would be appropriate. This par-four is the longest par-four on the course at 522 yards. The ideal position for the tee shot is on the left side, beyond the bunker that juts into the fairway. From there it's a long iron or fairway wood to the green. The fairway is mostly quite wide with very gentle undulations. There is a small bunker centered on the width of the green but about twenty yards short.

Number fourteen is 472 yards long, a little shorter than the previous hole but still quite substantial. The fairway has two bunkers on the right that are two hundred and fifty yards from the tee, and are about twenty yards long. The green is beside a lake on the right, hence the preferred route is from the left side of the fairway.

NUMBER SEVEN, A 187-YARD PAR-THREE

GOLF COURSES OF THE HIGH SIERRA

Number fifteen is a par-three, 221 yards long. There is water all along the left side and in front of the green. Six separate smallish bunkers are sprinkled around the green, and there is some awkward mounding behind the putting surface. It's a satisfying shot if you succeed; if you don't, be sure to miss toward the right side.

The sixteenth is a 396-yard par-four. At approximately 250 yards from the tee the fairway pinches in from the left and the right to a width of no more than fifteen yards. Beyond that it opens up again, making the choice ever so easy—stay short of the narrow waist or carry your drive past it.

Number seventeen, the last par-three, is 230 yards long and runs alongside an escarpment on the right. The green's orientation demands a shot directed at the left side with a fade. There's a very large bunker behind the green and a smaller one in front, but only slightly smaller. There also are two pot bunkers to fill out the list of potential problems.

On eighteen, a 451-yard par-four, a perfect drive can put you in middle-iron range of the green. But the shot is uphill, meaning that the exact distance is a mystery to most players. If it happens that you're between clubs, the safest play is not to the flag but to the right. This was exactly my predicament when, after a rare long drive, I hit a six-iron on line but short by a yard or two and ended up in the front bunker. I dropped another ball and hit a five-iron that flew into the back bunker. Such is golf for some of us.

Nevertheless, or should I say because of scenarios like that, this is a great finishing hole. For the players, it is a genuine test of their skills. For the spectators who gather on the patio in front of the clubhouse overlooking the green, it can provide some drama as well. It has the potential for greatness as well as disaster. Now, that's golf.

| HOLE | 1 | 2 | 3 | 4 | 5 | 6 | 7 | 8 | 9 | OUT | | 10 | 11 | 12 | 13 | 14 | 15 | 16 | 17 | 18 | IN | TOT | HCP | NET |
|---|---|---|---|---|---|---|---|---|---|---|---|---|---|---|---|---|---|---|---|---|---|---|---|---|
| | 462 | 631 | 196 | 383 | 484 | 578 | 187 | 357 | 452 | 3730 | | 600 | 345 | 551 | 522 | 472 | 221 | 396 | 230 | 451 | 3788 | 7518 | | |
| | 425 | 582 | 171 | 363 | 441 | 568 | 161 | 334 | 400 | 3445 | | 557 | 330 | 507 | 487 | 426 | 199 | 369 | 208 | 416 | 3499 | 6944 | | |
| | 407 | 564 | 139 | 349 | 411 | 500 | 138 | 318 | 386 | 3212 | | 540 | 270 | 493 | 429 | 408 | 171 | 355 | 182 | 397 | 3245 | 6457 | | |
| | 317 | 475 | 109 | 301 | 326 | 436 | 110 | 269 | 345 | 2688 | | 463 | 221 | 425 | 363 | 363 | 111 | 300 | 158 | 327 | 2731 | 5419 | | |
| MEN'S HCP | 7 | 1 | 13 | 11 | 5 | 3 | 15 | 17 | 9 | | | 2 | 16 | 6 | 8 | 4 | 12 | 18 | 14 | 10 | | | | |
| | | | | | | | | | | | | | | | | | | | | | | | | |
| PAR | 4 | 5 | 3 | 4 | 4 | 5 | 3 | 4 | 4 | 36 | | 5 | 4 | 5 | 4 | 4 | 3 | 4 | 3 | 4 | 36 | | | |
| | | | | | | | | | | | | | | | | | | | | | | | | |
| LADIES' HCP | 7 | 1 | 13 | 11 | 5 | 3 | 15 | 17 | 9 | | | 2 | 16 | 6 | 8 | 4 | 12 | 18 | 14 | 10 | | | | |
| DATE: | SCORER: | | | | | | | | | | | ATTEST: | | | | | | | | | | | | |

SQUAW VALLEY WAS FIRST NOTICED BY THE world when Alexander Cushing secured the 1960 Winter Olympics, beating out Innsbruck, Austria, the international favorite. At the time there were no facilities to speak of, but Cushing's Yankee know-how made it happen. Now Squaw Valley, also known as Olympic Valley, has developed a name that easily ranks with other ski resorts around the world.

That reputation was for the winter season when snow covers the ground. Summer was quite a different story until Lowe Enterprises came to town with the idea of building a hotel with a golf course attached. The hotel would blend into the hillside, and the golf course would occupy part of the mountainside and part of the meadow. More than half of the year this meadow is either covered by several feet of snow, and when it warms up in spring the runoff puts the meadow under water producing a wetlands. Then, during

# Resort at
# Squaw Creek

*6,931 yards, par 71*
*Architect: Robert Trent Jones, Jr.*
*Opened for play: 1991*
*Altitude: 6,247 feet*
*Head Professional: Eric Veraguth*

*THE THIRD HOLE, A 242-YARD PAR-THREE, IS CARVED INTO A STEEP MOUNTAINSIDE*

the summer months the water evaporates into the atmosphere. This was the natural cycle, and through the years many animals, large and small, lived and thrived in this meadow.

The meadow is several thousand acres large, of which the golf course uses a few hundred. Of the eighteen holes, eight have no contact with the wetlands, two have partial contact, and the remaining eight are totally surrounded by the marsh. Connecting the wetland holes is a unique system of wooden cart paths. The roadbed sits atop a series of columns that are driven into the wet ground every fifteen feet or so, allowing the marsh and its occupants to move and to continue living and breathing as one. Other than the noise created by golf carts driving on the paths, this was an elegant solution to the concerns of naturalists and a good one for the golfers as well.

Wetlands have mostly been thought of as "inconvenient puddles" for most of our history. It wasn't until organizations such as the Sierra Club, and individual naturalists who studied them, determined that they are an integral link in the fabric of our ecology. Now the push to respect and preserve these natural ecosystems has taken on an increasingly important role. And developers who build near, or indeed on them, have to present responsible plans.

This was one of the compelling reasons for the selection of Robert Trent Jones, Jr., as the architect for the golf course that would occupy part of the Squaw Creek Meadow. Besides being a very accomplished designer of golf courses around the world, Jones has demonstrated his respect for the environment as a past member and chairman of the California State Parks and Recreation Commission.

The permitting process for the development of a hotel

*OVERLEAF:*
*THE SQUAW CREEK MEADOW IN THE LATE AFTERNOON*

*THE SECOND HOLE AT THE TOP, NUMBER ONE IN THE MIDDLE, WITH A VIEW OF THE TENTH GREEN AT THE BOTTOM*

with a golf course can be long and arduous. This is especially so in California, where many state agencies and local committees have to be shown the plans, have to be sold on the benefits such a development will bring to the area, and convinced that there will not be a negative impact. The Lake Tahoe region seems to be especially sensitive to the effect increased traffic can bring to the once pristine lake and its surroundings. And in the case of the Squaw Creek meadow, the drinking water for locals and visitors alike comes from aquifers right below the proposed development.

Once the permits were granted, construction began, and in 1991 the golf course opened for play. But the environmental oversight is not finished. The TRC, Technical Review Committee, issued a sizable document called "CHAMP" that defines what can and cannot be done in terms of fertilizing the turf. Working hand in hand with the TRC, course superintendent John Heldman is constantly experimenting with organic fertilizers that will be less harmful to the environment. Twice a year the ground water is tested for contamination by the TRC. So far the golf course and hotel have proved to be extremely responsible citizens.

After rising through the ranks, Eric Veraguth now is the

head golf professional at the Resort at Squaw Creek. He succeeded Doug Flynn, who moved up the road to Whitehawk Golf Resort, and Bob Hickam, who is now Director of Golf at Old Greenwood. Eric's duties as head professional can be described very simply—make the course operate without problems. This includes managing the staff, taking care of the golf shop, supervising and working with the greenkeeper, taking care of the occasional faux pas....and so on and on. And since this is a resort hotel that hosts many conferences, there are many golf outings to accommodate. All have their own special needs, which Eric and his staff are only too happy to satisfy.

Sometimes the golf course is described as a links-style course, which would mean a seaside location and a base made of sand. The closest ocean is about one hundred and seventy-five miles due west, and the base is a marsh. What is probably meant is that the terrain of the meadow is flat and the wind that hurtles down over the mountains makes it necessary to keep the shots down....just like in Scotland.

The first tee is presided over by the statue of a golfer. Some say it was modeled after Bobby Jones, the architect. Well, I don't know about that, but I have heard a

rumor that should you touch his left shoe with the head of your driver before teeing up your ball, you will be in the fairway. Where your ball winds up may be quite another story.

The par-four first hole starts your round in a benign fashion. The ball first has to go through a fairly tight section of the fairway with trees left and right but opens up quite a bit in the landing area. There is a bunker on the right side that should be used for direction. The green is about twice as long as it is wide, has two levels and a small pot bunker at the right front. The second hole, also a par-four, runs parallel to the first in the opposite direction and is slightly longer. It curves gently to the left, with a bunker on the left that should be carried. The fairway opens up after that, but that bulge on the left side ought to be avoided since there are trees to deal with on that line. The green is of the same width as number one but quite a bit longer. There are traps left and right, with a smallish pot bunker behind the two-tiered putting surface.

*THE SIXTH, A 210-YARD PAR-THREE TAKES A CRISP SHOT TO REACH THE GREEN, ESPECIALLY INTO THE EVER PRESENT WIND*

All of the greens, though undulating and most with two or three plateaus, are easily read and are quite consistent. They are kept fast, usually measuring to a Stimpmeter speed of 8.

Number three is the first par-three. It is cut into the mountainside, making the hole appear even longer and narrower than its actual length of 242 yards. Nevertheless, it is a challenging hole with a prevailing wind usually helping out. The fourth is a straightforward, tree-lined par-five. The 554 yards of this hole can be accomplished with two great shots. This is the only hole that has home sites around the green, which is not too big and is surrounded by traps.

The fifth is the first hole out of the trees and into the meadow. It is a shortish par-four with the wetlands on the right. The landing area gets wider the closer you get to the green, but beware the marsh cutting across the fairway about ninety yards from the two-tiered green.

Number six is the resort's signature hole, and for good reason. It's over water from all five tee positions. Squaw Mountain dominates the background, and it usually plays into the prevailing wind coming off the mountain. This wind can be anything from zero to thirty knots or more. When you combine this with the 210-yard carry, you can only take solace in the fact that

*THE MEADOW IS PROTECTED FROM GOLF CART
TRAFFIC BY WOODEN CAUSEWAYS*

At this point, it might be appropriate to take a look back and enjoy the panoramic view of the meadow. Then start planning how the next nine holes need to be played. The tenth hole starts out surrounded by trees, but it doesn't take long before you're back in the marsh. This is a par-four of less than four hundred yards with a sliver of marsh on the left side and water beyond that. Eleven is slightly longer but stays with the theme.

The most forward tee boxes are mostly in front of forced carries, which does take away the exhilaration of a successful shot, but allows players who cannot fly the ball that far to enjoy the course as well.

Number twelve is made up of three separate and distinct areas—the teeing boxes, the landing area and the green with a small approach area in front. In between are the "natural" grasses and a lot of water. This par-four is 445 yards long and by most accounts should be the number one handicap hole, even though it quite often plays downwind. The par-five thirteenth climbs back into the trees, offering a much-appreciated respite

there is a bailout area to the left of the green.

The tee shot on the par-four seventh has to carry about a hundred and fifty yards of marsh before it finds the fairway. This hole also is not too long at 365 yards, but accuracy is not only desirable but essential. There are bunkers on the right side that should not come into play. Number eight is much the same, requiring a long carry from the tee over wetlands to a very generous landing zone, followed by an approach shot that also has to carry a sizable marshy area. This is the shortest par-four at 338 yards, but it's the number one handicap hole. The ninth, a narrow par-five of 514 yards, has a double dogleg, first turning gently to the right, then straight, and finally swinging left to the green. The green has three smallish bunkers protecting it, but it is the largest on the course.

from the marsh. It's not too long at 513 yards, but for most players it requires three shots to get to a large green. There is a combination of two bunkers on the right side, starting about one hundred yards in front of the putting surface and extending all the way to the green. Number fourteen is a lengthy par-three, coming back down the hill to a peanut-shaped green that is bunkered on the left and back. It's the ability to hit the ball 220 yards on line that's tested here.

It's back in the marsh for fifteen, which demands another forced carry, even from the forward tee. Not much trouble is designed into this 403 yard par-four, other than the problem of hitting a fairway that is hardly visible from the tee.

The sixteenth is a par-three of 204 yards, with a landing area about forty yards deep in front of the green. Seventeen is a par-four, 424 yards long, with wetlands cutting across the tee box and then again in front of the green. The second shot could be as long as 200 yards and has to carry this hazard, making the hole a great test. After all, this is the penultimate hole and energy may be waning.

The eighteenth has all the elements necessary in a great finishing hole. It is long, a 484-yard par-four, it has a long carry off the tee to a fairway that is not too wide, with water to the right and in front of the green, and it has greenside bunkers to catch the stray shot. On other courses, the finishing hole might be a par-five that allows players to be heroic and attempt to reach the green in two, striving for eagle or birdie. On this finishing hole, a few heroic shots are needed just to make par.

This is just a delightful golf course on which to spend an afternoon. That is, unless you attempt feats you're not capable of. Then the golf course will assert itself.

The only question that remains: on the first tee, did you touch the statue's left shoe?

| HOLE | GOLD Rated 72.6/Slope 143 | BLUE Rated 70.8/Slope 139 | WHITE Rated 68.3/Slope 125 | PAR | | | | | | HANDICAP | RED Rated 69.6/Slope 132 |
|---|---|---|---|---|---|---|---|---|---|---|---|
| 1 | 406 | 368 | 339 | 4 | | | | | | 11 | 305 |
| 2 | 430 | 404 | 379 | 4 | | | | | | 15 | 344 |
| 3 | 242 | 205 | 181 | 3 | | | | | | 17 | 150 |
| 4 | 554 | 525 | 495 | 5 | | | | | | 9 | 467 |
| 5 | 386 | 371 | 335 | 4 | | | | | | 13 | 281 |
| 6 | 210 | 176 | 153 | 3 | | | | | | 5 | 124 |
| 7 | 365 | 343 | 333 | 4 | | | | | | 7 | 286 |
| 8 | 338 | 318 | 290 | 4 | | | | | | 1 | 243 |
| 9 | 514 | 488 | 467 | 5 | | | | | | 3 | 436 |
| OUT | 3445 | 3198 | 2972 | 36 | | | | | | | 2636 |
| PLAYER | | | | | | | | | | | |
| 10 | 385 | 365 | 325 | 4 | | | | | | 10 | 300 |
| 11 | 402 | 387 | 349 | 4 | | | | | | 14 | 213 |
| 12 | 445 | 412 | 395 | 4 | | | | | | 6 | 346 |
| 13 | 513 | 496 | 480 | 5 | | | | | | 12 | 441 |
| 14 | 221 | 202 | 179 | 3 | | | | | | 18 | 126 |
| 15 | 403 | 378 | 348 | 4 | | | | | | 8 | 273 |
| 16 | 204 | 184 | 166 | 3 | | | | | | 16 | 124 |
| 17 | 429 | 407 | 385 | 4 | | | | | | 2 | 312 |
| 18 | 484 | 424 | 411 | 4 | | | | | | 4 | 326 |
| IN | 3486 | 3255 | 3038 | 35 | | | | | | | 2461 |
| TOT | 6931 | 6453 | 6010 | 71 | | | | | | | 5097 |
| HANDICAP | | | | | | | | | | | |
| NET SCORE | | | | | | | | | | | |
| DATE: | | SCORER: | | | | | ATTEST: | | | | |

OFTEN CALLED THE FATHER OF MODERN GOLF architecture, Robert Trent Jones is credited with designing or renovating more than five hundred golf courses around the world. There are Robert Trent Jones courses in forty-five states and thirty-five countries. His courses have hosted twenty-one U.S. Opens and twelve PGA Championships. Some of the better-known courses in his portfolio are Spyglass Hill in California, Bellerive and Old Warson in St. Louis, Hazeltine National in Minneapolis, Point O'Woods in Benton Harbor, Michigan, Shady Oaks in Fort Worth, the Houston Country Club, Coral Ridge in Fort Lauderdale, Tanglewood in Winston-Salem, the Dunes in Myrtle Beach, Robert Trent Jones International outside of Washington, D.C., Cotton Bay in the Bahamas, Port Royal in Bermuda, Ballybunion New in Ireland, Mauna Kea and Royal Kaanapali in Hawaii, Royal Golf Dar Es Salaam in Morocco, Cerromar and Dorado

# *Incline Village Golf Courses*

*CHAMPIONSHIP COURSE*

*7,106 yards, par 72*

*Architect: Robert Trent Jones*

*Opened for play: 1964*

*Course Renovation, 2004: Kyle Phillips*

*Altitude: 6,496 feet*

*Director of Golf: Cathy Jo Johnson*

*MOUNTAIN COURSE*

*3,519 yards, par 58*

*Architect: Robert Trent Jones, Jr.*

*Opened for play: 1968*

*Altitude: 6,857 feet*

*Head Professional: Angie Rodriguez*

Beach in Puerto Rico, and Valderrama in Spain. His first important work was a collaboration with Bobby Jones, who was not related, that created Peachtree in Atlanta in 1948. In 1974 he was chosen to design the first golf course ever planned for the Soviet Union. Jones may be just as well-known for his remodeling work at Augusta National, where he created the famous par-three sixteenth hole, Oakland Hills, Colonial and Southern Hills, Congressional, Olympic, Baltusrol, Oak Hill, all U.S. Open sites, as well as Firestone South and the Broadmoor. Jones was the original Open Doctor.

He studied at Cornell University, where, because he never graduated from high school, he was accepted as a special student. Since there was no specific course leading to a degree in golf course architecture, he designed his own curriculum, which included landscape architecture, hydraulics, surveying, agronomy, horticulture, economics, chemistry, public speaking, journalism and business law. All this to design and build golf courses….and in the case of Trent Jones, to make an historic career in the process.

Trent's philosophy was that "every hole should be a hard par and an easy bogey," an attitude reflected in most of his creations. Still, Jones was often accused, especially by professionals, of designing courses that were much too penal, too hard for ordinary humans. This concern was voiced by a member about Baltusrol Golf Club's fourth hole, a par-three over water to a two-tiered green that can play as long as 199 yards but is usually shorter for members. It was one of the holes Jones had remodeled for the 1954 U.S. Open. Mr. Jones agreed to meet his critic, along with C.P. Burgess, the tournament chairman, and Johnny Farrell, the head professional. Each of the three put his tee shot on the green, whereupon Jones struck a mashie shot that landed six feet short of the hole and hopped straightaway into the cup. "Gentlemen," Jones said, "I think the hole is eminently fair."

He traveled among the famous, creating a putting green at the White House for President Eisenhower as well as a golf hole at Camp David, the presidential retreat, that has three different tees. He knew all the movers and shakers around the world.

Jones passed away on June 14, 2000, but his astonishing legacy will live forever.

The Incline Village course is designed in what might be

NUMBER FIVE, A 219-YARD PAR-THREE

*THE SECOND HOLE'S GREEN AT TOP, AND THE FAIRWAY AS SEEN FROM THE TEE WHICH IS SURROUNDED BY TALL, DARK TREES*

called "the Jones Style." There are no trendy features, no superfluous appendices, just a straightforward, muscular golf course that upon closer examination has a lot of intricacies, a course that will test all aspects of a player's arsenal, especially his mind. It mostly asks for the ability to hit the ball fairly long off the tee. The fairways in the landing areas are usually quite generous and always feature a large bunker or bunkers to show the way. The greens are well-bunkered, usually with an entrance for a running shot. Some greens are relatively flat, others have undulations that will make you cry uncle if you don't get your approach close. The shape of the greens might be anything, from circular to oval to peanut shaped, always providing interesting hole locations that might be just behind a bunker, or out in the middle but beside a ridge. The greens are fair, mostly rising toward the back to accept long shots or level when a high approach will be the norm. This course, with its nuances, can be played often without it becoming bland. It is a course with character, a course for competitions. This is especially true since the golf course reopened for play in 2005 after extensive renovations were performed.

There came a time when it was quite evident that the old clubhouse had served its function and there needed to be a new structure to satisfy the needs of the future. When this was talked about, the renovation of the golf course itself was also tabled. Kyle Phillips, who before opening his own shop had worked for Robert Trent Jones, Jr., was retained by the Board of Trustees to come up with a master plan. The logistics of this was one of the major items, and the board decided to close the course, build a new clubhouse and renovate the course. Obviously not a light decision, but in hindsight the proper one.

Kyle Phillips gained an international reputation when Kingsbarns Golf Links, just south of St. Andrews in Scotland, opened in 2000. He also designed Golf Eichenheim in Kitzbuehel, half-way between Innsbruck and Salzburg, in the Austrian Alps, most noted for the Hahnenkamm downhill ski race course and Franz Klammer's spectacular feats.

The renovation of the Championship Course at Incline Village was mainly one of restoration. Over the years, bunkers had deteriorated and, with the improvement in equipment, they were sometimes in the wrong places. Internal modifications had pushed the course enough away from the original design that a restoration became a plausible choice for the historically minded management. One significant change that was made involved the "shaving down" of landing areas, which

enabled the player to see the tee shot land. The tee boxes also were changed from the original, enlarging and squaring them for a more formal look. A great benefit to the first-time player at Incline is that the sides of the tee boxes can actually be used to align your shot. The size of these tees is legendary. On the eleventh hole, the tee is a full sixty five yards long; admittedly it accommodates three tees, but still it's long enough to land a glider.

The new clubhouse, built while the course was being renovated, is named "The Chateau." An impressive structure overlooking the first and ninth holes, it wears many hats. On the upper level there is a conference area that can be shaped to satisfy the needs of varied groups, a restaurant and a bar, as well as the sales office. Many kinds of functions have found this a fitting place, with weddings at the ninth green becoming very popular. A balcony running the entire width of the building is especially suitable for watching the action on the ninth green and the first and third tees. On the lower level, golf is trump. This is where the golf shop, the starter and golf staff offices are.

The first hole, a par-four of 432 yards, provides the proper

*OVERLEAF:*
*THE UPHILL NINTH, A 413-YARD PAR-FOUR*

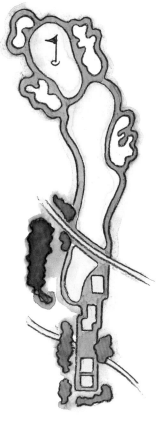

perspective. Right away the course demands your attention. In front of the tee is a brook gurgling away. Not in any way does it come into play here, but the thought is planted, and like hazards play a role in intimidation and club selection later on. Looking up, there are bunkers on the left and right side, with about thirty yards of fairway between. Beyond, about seventy-five yards in front of the green, is another brook crossing the fairway. The green itself is long and wide, gently undulating, with bunkers on both sides.

The next hole is a 494-yard par-five that starts out through a sixty-yard chute slightly downhill to a broad fairway. A small pot bunker on the left is followed by a much larger monster. Fronting the green is a creek, with a bed so big that trees grow in it. Most times this shot is into the wind coming off the lake. The green has two levels, and there's a single bunker behind. The other par-five on the front nine is number four. It is a downhill monster of 621 yards, and as one might expect, it is the most difficult hole on the course

Number three, par-four and 423 yards, is the first of two holes that offer a straight tee shot and a second shot to the green that is more or less at a ninety-degree angle. The other is the sixteenth. Neither hole offers a shortcut; the best route is to play

*TRAPS, TRAPS, AND MORE TRAPS ABOVE,*
*AND THE SEVENTEENTH GREEN AT LEFT*

*ONE OF TWO GREENSIDE BUNKERS AT THE FIRST HOLE, WITH THE SECOND FAIRWAY BEYOND*

*THE FOURTH GREEN*

the holes as designed—a long, straight tee shot, favoring the right side on both, then a short iron to the green.

Numbers six and seven run parallel to Tahoe Boulevard and are straightaway holes in the four-hundred-yard vicinity. Not so on the ninth. This is a hole that goes up a hill that could be used as a ski slope during winter. Looking up from the tee, the fairway appears completely blocked by sand. The fairway does go between them, but the damage to your psyche may already be done. A prevailing wind is at your back, helping a little. The green is flanked by two strategic bunkers and is relatively level.

The par-threes are all fairly long, the shortest 175 yards, the longest 219 yards and the other two just more than 200 yards. Number five is the longest, and to make things worse, it's into the wind most of the time. There is also water in the form of a pond that stretches halfway across the fairway. The eighth is the shortest and easiest, but the tee shot has to go between some very tall trees. The fifteenth requires a long shot over a chasm to a mere sliver of a green. Seventeen is similar.

There are about sixty bunkers on the course. Their primary function is that of directional road signs, but they must be respected and avoided. They come in a variety of shapes, some round, some oval, most resembling sea monsters with many arms, all reaching out for your Titleist. Some have very shallow faces, others are steep enough and high enough to require a sideways exit. Some are very small, others are in two time zones. The only common element is sand.

The back nine starts with an uphill 398 yard par-four, is followed by a 514 yard par-five that might be reached in two. The theme for all these holes has been established: inviting fairways, with bunkers on both sides in the landing areas and strategically placed around the greens. Even though there is a sameness to the ingredients, the holes themselves offer quite different challenges.

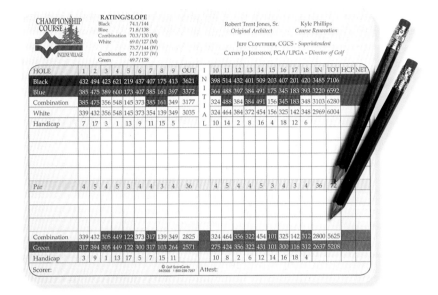

**CHAMPIONSHIP COURSE — INCLINE VILLAGE**

RATING/SLOPE
Black 74.1/144
Blue 71.8/138
Combination 70.3/130 (M)
White 69.0/127 (M) 73.7/144 (W)
Combination 71.7/137 (W)
Green 69.7/128

Robert Trent Jones, Sr. - *Original Architect*
Kyle Phillips - *Course Renovation*
Jeff Clouthier, CGCS - *Superintendent*
Cathy Jo Johnson, PGA/LPGA - *Director of Golf*

| HOLE | 1 | 2 | 3 | 4 | 5 | 6 | 7 | 8 | 9 | OUT | | 10 | 11 | 12 | 13 | 14 | 15 | 16 | 17 | 18 | IN | TOT | HCP | NET |
|---|---|---|---|---|---|---|---|---|---|---|---|---|---|---|---|---|---|---|---|---|---|---|---|---|
| Black | 432 | 494 | 423 | 621 | 219 | 437 | 407 | 175 | 413 | 3621 | I | 398 | 514 | 432 | 401 | 509 | 203 | 407 | 201 | 420 | 3485 | 7106 | | |
| Blue | 385 | 475 | 389 | 600 | 173 | 407 | 385 | 161 | 397 | 3372 | N | 364 | 488 | 397 | 384 | 491 | 175 | 345 | 183 | 393 | 3220 | 6592 | | |
| Combination | 385 | 475 | 356 | 548 | 145 | 373 | 385 | 161 | 349 | 3177 | I | 324 | 488 | 384 | 384 | 491 | 156 | 345 | 183 | 348 | 3103 | 6280 | | |
| White | 339 | 432 | 356 | 548 | 145 | 373 | 354 | 139 | 349 | 3035 | T | 324 | 464 | 384 | 372 | 454 | 156 | 325 | 142 | 348 | 2969 | 6004 | | |
| Handicap | 7 | 17 | 3 | 1 | 13 | 9 | 11 | 15 | 5 | | I | 10 | 14 | 2 | 8 | 16 | 4 | 18 | 12 | 6 | | | | |
| | | | | | | | | | | | A | | | | | | | | | | | | | |
| Par | 4 | 5 | 4 | 5 | 3 | 4 | 4 | 3 | 4 | 36 | L | 4 | 5 | 4 | 4 | 5 | 3 | 4 | 3 | 4 | 36 | 72 | | |
| Combination | 339 | 432 | 305 | 449 | 122 | 373 | 317 | 139 | 349 | 2825 | | 324 | 464 | 356 | 322 | 454 | 101 | 325 | 142 | 312 | 2800 | 5625 | | |
| Green | 317 | 394 | 305 | 449 | 122 | 300 | 317 | 103 | 264 | 2571 | | 275 | 424 | 356 | 322 | 431 | 101 | 300 | 116 | 312 | 2637 | 5208 | | |
| Handicap | 3 | 9 | 1 | 11 | 17 | 5 | 7 | 15 | 11 | | | 10 | 8 | 2 | 6 | 12 | 14 | 16 | 18 | 4 | | | | |
| Scorer: | | | | | | | | | | | | | | | | | | | | Attest: | | | | |

© Golf ScoreCards 04/2005 1 800-236-7267

Number eighteen, is a downhill dogleg par-four of 420 yards, might be a fine hole in the middle of the course, but it lacks some of the drama usually associated with great finishing holes. The tee shot crosses two river beds and is aimed at a bunker on the right. From there, the green is below your feet, surrounded by three bunkers. Birdie is a distinct possibility.

Even though there are no official championships hosted by Incline Village, competition is alive and well here. No less than five separate clubs call this course home and compete weekly. And who knows, with the new and improved look crafted by Kyle Phillips, perhaps a championship will be conducted soon on the Championship Course.

ROBERT TRENT JONES, JR. DID NOT FALL FAR FROM THE tree. Bobby and his brother Rees both became golf architects. They both cut their teeth under the guidance of their father. But Bobby eventually decided to go out on his own, and California seemed a great place to explore. He opened his shop in Palo Alto in the mid 1960s and has designed 220 courses around the world since, with many more in the works. As with his father, there doesn't seem to be a bad one among them. Courses his firm takes credit for include The Links at Spanish Bay, Poppy

Hills Golf Course, Pelikan Bay, Bodega Harbour Golf Links, Desert Dunes, Monarch Beach Golf Links, Rancho San Marcos Golf Club, The Resort at Squaw Creek, Shoreline Golf Links and Silverado Country Club South....and that's just a few he has done in California.

Not to mention the Incline Village Mountain Course, an executive course just up the mountainside from the Championship Course. Overlooking Lake Tahoe, this little course, since it is a few hundred feet higher, offers in some instances even more dramatic views of Lake Tahoe than does the championship layout.

Executive golf courses, also known as par-threes, or simply as short courses, are becoming more and more popular with segments of the golfing public. The myth that they're miniature golf courses without the windmills is just that, a myth. The Mountain Course has all the ingredients of the Championship Course without the need to carry a driver. Short courses provide a place for beginning golfers, active older golfers who simply can't carry two-hundred-yard waste areas, and those who need to sharpen their short game. Another factor is that most of the new courses designed today seem to have a need to out-design and out-distance each other. In Singapore there is a new

*THE THIRD, AS PERFECT A COMPOSITION AS AN ARTIST COULD MUSTER*

NUMBER TWELVE AT TOP LEFT, THE FOURTEENTH AT TOP RIGHT, AND THE EIGHTEENTH GREEN WITH FAIRWAY AT THE BOTTOM

course with a par-six hole that crosses a river twice. Not everyone thinks of that as a great time.

This course is a par 58, 3,519 yards long from the back tees and about five hundred yards shorter from the front tees. The unofficial course record is a 52, by several players who did not leave their names. There are four par-four holes, the longest of which is number eighteen, one yard shy of four hundred yards. The average length of the fourteen par-threes is one hundred and fifty yards. Just by coincidence this seems to be the distance at which most golfers, playing the longer courses, would love to increase their accuracy. This would be the perfect venue for these players to hone their mid-iron game without the distraction of looking for their ball in the left or right rough after hitting a driver.

The greens are more or less the same size as on the Championship Course and have gentle undulations. Some are tiered but are easily read, and they are kept somewhat slower than the greens on the championship course. Bunkers are actually more plentiful, though smaller and not as severe. Most greens are in front of a dense forest background, making the target easily seen.

This course remains a favorite with groups of golfers who want to get together for a fun-filled afternoon, and perhaps some good shots. The clubhouse stands ready to entertain these folks afterward, and the staff stands ready not to listen to their tall stories, which usually are plentiful, but to help them relax.

A few small changes have been made since the course was opened for play—the first and fourth holes were switched, a bunker was added at the eighteenth green, and some cart paths were laid. Other than that, the course is exactly as it was in 1968. Why fool with perfection?

Jones has said that this is his favorite short course, and somehow that's not hard to believe.

**Mountain Course**
INCLINE VILLAGE LAKE TAHOE

**COURSE RATING/SLOPE**

|  | Men | Women |
|---|---|---|
| Back Tee | 58.0/105 | 60.2/97 |
| Forward Tee |  | 57.2/91 |

**Cathy Jo Johnson, PGA/LPGA**
*Director of Golf*
**Angie Rodriguez**
*PGA Head Professional*
**Shaun Riley**
*Golf Course Superintendent*

| HOLE | 1 | 2 | 3 | 4 | 5 | 6 | 7 | 8 | 9 | OUT | 10 | 11 | 12 | 13 | 14 | 15 | 16 | 17 | 18 | IN | TOT | HCP | NET |
|---|---|---|---|---|---|---|---|---|---|---|---|---|---|---|---|---|---|---|---|---|---|---|---|
| BACK | 346 | 136 | 113 | 135 | 375 | 130 | 125 | 200 | 158 | 1718 | 185 | 179 | 140 | 298 | 185 | 117 | 175 | 123 | 399 | 1801 | 3519 | | |
| HANDICAP | 5 | 9 | 17 | 13 | 7 | 11 | 15 | 1 | 3 | | 6 | 8 | 12 | 10 | 2 | 16 | 18 | 14 | 4 | | | | |
| PAR | 4 | 3 | 3 | 3 | 4 | 3 | 3 | 3 | 3 | 29 | 3 | 3 | 3 | 4 | 3 | 3 | 3 | 3 | 4 | 29 | 58 | | |
| FORWARD | 340 | 116 | 105 | 113 | 325 | 112 | 125 | 178 | 114 | 1528 | 127 | 150 | 124 | 275 | 158 | 90 | 114 | 105 | 358 | 1501 | 3029 | | |
| HANDICAP | 3 | 17 | 15 | 9 | 5 | 13 | 11 | 1 | 7 | | 4 | 14 | 8 | 6 | 10 | 18 | 16 | 12 | 2 | | | | |
| TARGET TIME | :14 | :24 | :34 | :44 | :58 | 1:08 | 1:18 | 1:30 | 1:40 | | 1:52 | 2:02 | 2:12 | 2:26 | 2:36 | 2:46 | 2:56 | 3:06 | 3:20 | | | | |
| SCORER: | | | | | | | | | ATTEST: | | | | | | | | DATE: | | | | | | |

© Golf ScoreCards 09/2005 1-800-238-7267

AT THE SOUTH SHORE OF LAKE TAHOE, JUST A few hundred yards from the California state line, is the discreet entrance to Edgewood Tahoe. In the shadow of Heavenly Mountain ski resort and the tall buildings of the Nevada casinos, it adds another star to the star-filled firmament that is Lake Tahoe.

John C. Fremont, an explorer, was the first non-native man to see Lake Tahoe and to record that event on February 14, 1844. As it happened, it was by accident. He and his party were actually looking for the mythical Buenaventura River described by some geographers and said to flow into either the Gulf of Mexico, or San Francisco Bay.

Lake Tahoe had many names in its early history. Fremont initially had called it Lake Bonpland, honoring a French explorer and botanist. This did not achieve general usage, nor did Mountain Lake, also a name used by Fremont. In 1853 California was a new

# *Edgewood Tahoe*

*7,445 yards, par 72*

*Architect: George Fazio*

*Opened for play: 1968*

*Course Renovation, since 1992: Tom Fazio*

*Altitude: 6,246 feet*

*Head Professional: Randy Fox*

*THE EIGHTEENTH GREEN AT DUSK*

state and had an official mapmaker who named it Lake Bigler after the third governor of California. But, alas, this name was not generally accepted either. In 1861 there was an attempt to change it to Tula Tulia. The final name and its acceptance were spearheaded by William Henry Knight, a surveyor whose maps eventually were used by the Land Office in Washington, D.C., and who admired the region. Tahoe is an Indian name that had been used by the natives long before Fremont ever saw the lake.

The Pony Express was the "overnight" delivery service of the time. It employed daredevils, carrying their famous leather pouches, who would ride their mounts to exhaustion and only stop to exchange them at relay stations for a fresh one. Friday's Station was the most western of these stations and was founded by Friday Burke and Jim Small in 1860. This was the home station for a rider named Pony Bob Haslem, who once rode 380 miles on horseback uninterrupted, a feat still marveled at today.

Friday's Station, still stands in the vicinity of Edgewood Tahoe's fifth green, and was part of the property purchased by the Park family in 1896. It is hard to imagine today, with all the concrete, asphalt and steel that make up South Lake Tahoe, that this land was used for grazing cattle. But that was the business of the Park family then and still today—it operates a cattle

*NUMBER SIX IS A 434-YARD PAR-FOUR FROM THE TEE ABOVE,*
*WITH A SLIGHTLY CLOSER LOOK OF THE GREEN AT RIGHT*

ranch in the Carson Valley, about twenty miles east of Edgewood. In the early sixties, two generations later, Brooks Park was running the family business. On the suggestion of Del Webb, who owned the Sahara Tahoe, Brooks made the decision to build a golf course to complement the hotel. Brooks knew little about golf, but Webb knew a fellow named George Fazio, who he thought would do a great job of designing a golf course.

George Fazio was born in Norristown, Pennsylvania, on November 14, 1912, the same year that Sam Snead, Byron Nelson and Ben Hogan came into the world. Young George

NUMBER NINE GREEN

crash, won, and Fazio eventually went on to become a giant in the field of golf course architecture.

By all accounts, Fazio was a man who paid attention to the smallest details yet enjoyed the grand scale of golf course design—a valuable mix of talents indeed. While playing he always wore a white cap and tie, had an easy-going manner or was a driven autocrat, depending on who you listened to. Asked once what he had learned about golf architecture, he replied. "I don't think I'm any good at it." Smiling, he continued, "But I don't see anybody else who's better." As a designer, George Fazio developed a reputation for blending his golf courses seamlessly into the landscape. His bunkering, at the time, was considered creative, even unique. Besides Edgewood Tahoe, some of the golf courses Fazio designed include Moselem Springs in Pennsylvania, Butler National in Illinois and Jupiter Hills in Florida.

became acquainted with golf by caddying at a nearby country club. He was of slight build and at first did not excel at the game. Since at that time there were no instruction books or tapes, he took it on himself to analyze the golf swing, and eventually became a top-level player on the professional tour. He won the 1946 Canadian Open, lost the 1947 Bing Crosby tournament in a playoff with Ed Furgol, had several other runner-up finishes and wound up in the famous U.S. Open playoff with Ben Hogan and Lloyd Mangrum at Merion in 1950. Hogan, not long out of a hospital bed after his near-fatal car

Fazio was never quite satisfied with his own work, endlessly refining his designs. In 1964, an eighteen-year-old Tom Fazio came to work for his uncle and quickly showed promise as a coming star in the field. He easily acquired the skills needed to put a design to paper and then execute it in the field. So it is fitting that Tom Fazio should take on the responsibility of

PREVIOUS PAGES:
THE SIXTEENTH, EASILY ONE OF THE MOST BEAUTIFUL HOLES IN GOLF

frequent renovations at Edgewood Tahoe. For the first thirty years of the course's life, improvements that mainly kept the course abreast of ever-improving equipment as well as player enjoyment were handled internally. In 1990 Tom Fazio toured the course for the first time since 1968, and it was decided that his design firm would regularly evaluate and propose changes. Now there is talk of a master plan that would address changes for the next decade.

Competition, in fact just the simple act of keeping score, is one of the most defining attributes in golf. It is, after all, the way a player measures up against a course or against the competition of the moment. To this end, Edgewood Tahoe has hosted several important tournaments.

In 1980, Edgewood Tahoe was the site of the U.S. Amateur Public Links Championship won by Jodie Mudd of Louisville, Kentucky with a 9 and 8 victory over Richard Gordon. Mudd was one of 4,416 competitors vying for top honors. This was the first time a USGA competition was held in Nevada. In 1985, Miller Barber won his second consecutive Senior Open Championship with a score of three under 285. Roberto De Vicenzo, who was the victor of this tournament in 1980, was runner-up, four strokes behind. Several American

Junior Golf Association tournaments, whose entrants include the likes of Tiger Woods, Phil Mickelson and John Daly, have been conducted there.

Since 1990, one of the more popular events has found a home at Edgewood Tahoe. The American Century Celebrity Golf tournament is a nationally televised 54-hole tournament that attracts celebrities from the world of entertainment as well as sport. In 2005, former NFL quarterback Joe Tolliver was victorious. Other celebrities competing, and we'll only mention a few, were Michael Jordan, Donald Trump, Jimmy Connors, Charles Barkley, Jerry Rice, Rush Limbaugh, Dan Marino and Bode Miller. Miller, of course, is well known here in the High Sierra for his achievements on skis. The tournament has a purse of half a million dollars, with one hundred thousand going to the winner. However, in order to preserve their "amateur status," most competitors donate their winnings to a charity.

This golf course is primarily a venue for the visiting golfer, but Edgewood Tahoe does have two golf clubs that call it home. One is for men, with about a hundred members, the other for women, a somewhat smaller group. With a large waiting list ready to join, these clubs are kept small on purpose to

preserve the intimacy of these tightly-knit groups.

Edgewood Tahoe requires distance off the tee, coupled with accuracy to challenge the winds blowing off the lake. It darts in and out of the forest, with views of the surrounding mountains on virtually all holes. The greens are seeded in poa annua, are undulating in nature, and in most cases are severely bunkered. The fairway grass is a mixture of bluegrass, rye grass and poa annua.

The first is one of the easier holes on this golf course. It is 436 yards long with a fairly wide fairway and a large green, giving all players a chance to get the game in gear. Number two, at 417 yards is just a little shorter than the first hole, is also a par-four, requires a tee shot directed to the right side of the sloping fairway to set up a good shot to the green.

Numbers three and four are two consecutive par-five's of 599 yards and 572 yards respectively. The third curves majestically to the right, culminating at an elevated green surrounded on three sides by tall pines. The fourth is a straight piece of real estate until the approach to the green. The last one hundred yards of the fairway are flanked by a stream on the right. Farther to the right is a landing area with a huge bunker beyond.

*WIND IS OFTEN A FACTOR ON THE SEVENTEENTH, A 207-YARD PAR-THREE*

*LOOKING TOWARD THE CLUBHOUSE FROM THE THIRD FAIRWAY*

THE TENTH GREEN WITH ADJOINING WATER HAZARD AS SEEN FROM THE FIRST FAIRWAY

The choice for the second shot is whether to go straight toward the hole and stay in the main fairway or go to the right, which will provide a favorable angle to some hole locations. The green has a variety of interesting places to put the cup.

Number five is the first par-three, 220 yards long. Two bunkers guard the green, and in between the traps and at the left side of the green is a lone, ominous pine, somewhat blocking the entrance to the green.

The par-four sixth is 442 yards long. From an elevated tee the fairway looms large, making the second shot a bit of a surprise, because there is water on the right and bunkers all along the left. The green itself is surrounded by trees with a small opening in front. The next hole, a 169-yard par-three, offers more of the same, with trees surrounding the green on three sides. The green has three small traps on its left side, and a large horseshoe-shaped bunker on the right, around which the green wraps. A flag behind this bunker could be tough to get at.

The eighth is a par-four of 458-yards. The California-Nevada state line runs in between the eighth green and the ninth tee. The ninth is a 461-yard par-four that doglegs to the right. Number ten's fairway, a 441-yard par-four, first turns to the right and then to the left, with left bunkers that are eventu-

ally replaced by the lake, which continues on to the green. The tee shot at the 407-yard par-four eleventh travels from the darkness deep in the forest to a bright fairway. The green is guarded by a bunker on the right and a tall pine short of the putting surface. Number twelve is a par-three, 205 yards long, with a large bunker in front of the green that is fairly wide but not too deep.

Number thirteen is a par-four 434 yards long that doglegs to the right, with two bunkers in front of the green virtually

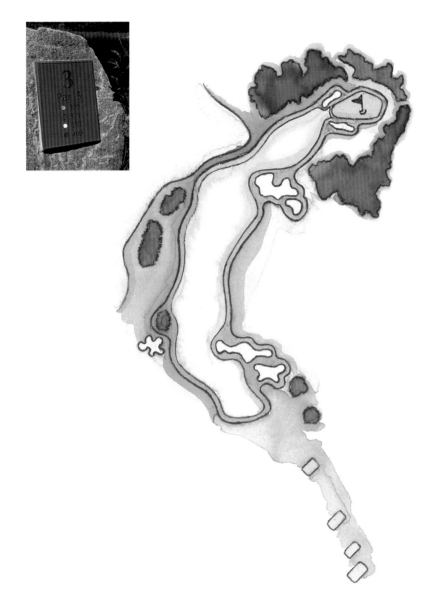

eliminating the opportunity for a run-up approach. The tees on the 447-yard par-four fourteenth are deep in the trees, with the fairway in the open, beckoning below. The lake will keep you company all the way to the green, which has a single bunker on the right side.

Number fifteen, is not too long at 394 yards, but it goes uphill and the second shot will have to carry a bunker that extends all the way across the front of the green. This style of bunkering will be seen again on the next two holes.

The sixteenth is a hole that, while you are standing on the tee, makes you savor the thought of what's ahead. It's a par-five of 564 downhill yards. The complete hole is visible, sloping down to the lake. There seem to be no real problems. But a large tree on the right center of the fairway looms large, quite often gathering in the tee shot and then blocking the next. From this vantage point there are bunkers literally all around the green, making it almost impossible to run the second shot onto the putting surface. A bunker that stretches across the front about fifty yards short of the green must be carried to reach the fifty yard deep peanut-shaped green.

Number seventeen, a par-three of 207 yards, sits in a most beautiful setting smack on the lake shore. The wind is often in your face from the right quarter, so choosing the proper club is critical. We're used to having bunkers front the greens by now, so this horseshoe-shaped bunker in front of this green shouldn't be much of a surprise. There are also two bunkers behind the green. Should you be in one of those, have a look back toward the tee and enjoy the view of the lake.

Sadly recognizing that the round is coming to a close, the eighteenth offers a straight away par-five of 572 yards. Reachable in two for ultra-long hitters, the green curves around a pond, reducing the opening considerably, and sports two bunkers behind and one on the right. A large stretch of sand, the Lake Tahoe beach, runs along most of the second half of the fairway. The pond by the green is actually part of a filtration system, cleansing golf-course water before it enters Lake Tahoe.

The clubhouse dominates the view as you close in on the final green. Although part of the master plan, it was not started until the golf course was completed and ready for play. During those first long months, the golf shop and other golf operations were managed out of a trailer. Brooks Park wanted to build the clubhouse along Highway 50, where there would be more exposure to potential clientele passing by. George Fazio argued and convinced him that a presence on the very edge of the lake

would be in the long-term interest of the development. Now that the clubhouse and the golf course have become part of the established landscape, we know that George Fazio could not have been more correct.

The routing of these eighteen holes also has stood the test of time, giving wonderful enjoyment to thousands of men and women over the years.

| HOLE | Rating/Slope | 1 | 2 | 3 | 4 | 5 | 6 | 7 | 8 | 9 | OUT | 10 | 11 | 12 | 13 | 14 | 15 | 16 | 17 | 18 | IN | TOT | HCP | NET |
|---|---|---|---|---|---|---|---|---|---|---|---|---|---|---|---|---|---|---|---|---|---|---|---|---|
| GOLD | 75.3/144 | 436 | 417 | 599 | 572 | 220 | 442 | 169 | 458 | 461 | 3774 | 441 | 407 | 205 | 434 | 447 | 391 | 564 | 207 | 572 | 3671 | 7445 | | |
| BLUE | 72.6/139 | 402 | 393 | 575 | 520 | 188 | 398 | 161 | 420 | 433 | 3490 | 413 | 372 | 187 | 425 | 406 | 362 | 547 | 175 | 501 | 3388 | 6878 | | |
| WHITE | 70.2/131 | 370 | 362 | 558 | 459 | 152 | 368 | 149 | 377 | 414 | 3209 | 383 | 328 | 167 | 387 | 388 | 341 | 533 | 140 | 489 | 3156 | 6365 | | |
| RED | 71.3/136 | 343 | 322 | 469 | 403 | 131 | 352 | 112 | 315 | 399 | 2846 | 353 | 259 | 127 | 344 | 334 | 309 | 451 | 107 | 437 | 2721 | 5567 | | |
| | | | | | | | | | | | | | | | | | | | | | | | | |
| | | | | | | | | | | | | | | | | | | | | | | | | |
| PAR | | 4 | 4 | 5 | 5 | 3 | 4 | 3 | 4 | 4 | 36 | 4 | 4 | 3 | 4 | 4 | 4 | 5 | 3 | 5 | 36 | 72 | | |
| | | | | | | | | | | | | | | | | | | | | | | | | |
| | | | | | | | | | | | | | | | | | | | | | | | | |
| MEN'S HCP | | 13 | 15 | 1 | 9 | 11 | 5 | 17 | 7 | 3 | | 6 | 12 | 10 | 2 | 4 | 16 | 8 | 18 | 14 | | | | |
| WOMEN'S HCP | | 9 | 13 | 5 | 11 | 17 | 1 | 15 | 7 | 3 | | 4 | 16 | 12 | 2 | 8 | 14 | 6 | 18 | 10 | | | | |

DATE: _____  SCORER: _____  ATTEST: _____

MAMMOTH LAKES IS THE HOME OF THE SIERRA Star Golf Club. At an altitude of a little more than eight thousand feet, it is the highest golf course in the High Sierra. Mammoth Lakes is a thriving community, with construction of new homes and condominiums visible wherever you look, even though there is constant earthquake danger and Mammoth Mountain is a volcano—dormant, but a volcano nonetheless.

There is not much known about the earliest people who inhabited the area. The first settlers actually only passed through on their way to California and didn't keep records. What is known, though, is that the Paiute tribe hunted and foraged on the eastern slope of the Sierra Nevada, and had a presence in what is now Mammoth Lakes. The first real settlers were prospectors, a transient population that drifted down from Virginia City and other places in the north whenever there was news of precious metals in the area. But

# *Sierra Star Golf Club*

*6,708 yards, par 70*

*Architect: Cal Olson*

*Opened for play: 1999*

*Altitude: 8,040 feet*

*Head Professional: Dave Schacht*

THE EIGHTEENTH, A RARE PAR-THREE FINISHING HOLE

*NUMBER FOUR*

has become very popular in the summer. There are slightly more than seven thousand year-round residents, and with about eighty-five hundred rental units available, the town can swell to more than thirty thousand on some weekends.

The Sierra Star course was built by Intrawest Corporation, which was striving to make Mammoth Lakes a four-season destination, fashioned after other developments with which they had been involved. Whistler/Blackcomb in British Columbia and Copper Mountain in Colorado are two examples. Cal Olson was retained to design the course, and after two years of cutting trees to accommodate fairways and greens, the course opened for play in 1999.

The course starts out in a slightly cramped fashion with a shortish par-four, followed by a par-three that is so short you can almost read putts from the tee. This was dictated by the land available. But then the course opens up and shows its true character. Tree-lined fairways, at times quite narrow, bend gently first in this direction and then that, below some of the best mountainscapes anywhere. The holes present different challenges, each one more picturesque than the last. The final two holes, the last a par-three, again seem to be squeezed into the space available. There are four tee locations on each hole, and

as soon as that proved to be a myth, those folks packed their bags and evaporated into thin air.

The modern history of the town is equally hazy. Without much fanfare or reason, people gathered in the meadow, built homes and somehow made a living. Then in 1937, when a modern highway was built into Mammoth Lakes from highway 395, bypassing the existing settlement, the town literally picked up and moved to its present location.

Now it is a community totally committed to tourism. There is skiing in the winter and, amongst other activities, golf

*THE THIRTEENTH COMBINES ALL THE BEST OF HIGH SIERRA GOLF*

*THE SIXTEENTH GREEN AT TOP AND NUMBER FOUR FAIRWAY AT BOTTOM*

since there is an almost thirteen hundred-yard difference between the black and red tees, with blue and white tees in between, it is important that you choose the proper tee to suit your particular game.

Dave Schacht, the head professional, says, "I recommend you check your ego at the door when you come to play here. There aren't many holes where the driver comes into play; careful placement is the key on this course." Sage advice.

The fairways are planted in a mixture of fescue and rye grass and for the most part have gentle undulations, only on occasion causing a tricky sidehill or downhill lie.

Jon Cook is the greenkeeper responsible for the beautiful shape this busy course is in. Continually working toward the lofty goal of perfection can be arduous at this altitude, where snow falls are legendary. Cook is also responsible for the bear sculptures seen around the course, which he carves during the winter, adding a whimsical theme to the layout. Did you notice the paw prints? There will probably be no interference from bears in the flesh, but it should be noted that this is their natural habitat. Up in the sky you might also see a hawk or two, circling in the thermals.

The 368-yard first is a little downhill and a bit on the nar-

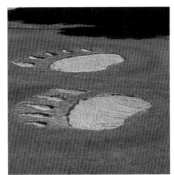

*A CONSTANT COMPANION ON YOUR JOURNEY AROUND THE COURSE*

row side. The green is fronted by an "environmentally sensitive" area, and once over it, this particular green is easy to read. Since there is no driving range but a great putting green, you'll also have no problem reading the other greens to come. They do need to be understood, though, since there are some very subtle breaks. The average size of the greens is about fifty-five-hundred square feet and is planted in bent grass.

The second hole has a false front, rejecting all shots short of the actual green. Ever so short at 118 yards, this par-three nevertheless is challenging. Maybe we all ought to practice hitting a teed-up ball with a sand wedge more often. The green is undulating, and putting can be difficult from some places.

The next four holes are lengthy par-fours, all in excess of four hundred yards. From the back tees, number three is 413

yards, four is 440 yards, five is 424 yards and the longest is number six at 469 yards. Whether at sea level or at eight thousand feet, the sixth would take two solid shots to get home in regulation. It is a long straight hole, with bunkers at strategic locations where errant shots might wind up. Off the tee, there is plenty of room on the right side of the fairway, which is also the suggested place since a shot to the green needs to come in from that side. There are several bunkers in front of and beside the green, leaving only a sliver of grass to bounce the ball onto the green. The green itself slopes dramatically up toward the back, helping to stop a low shot, but creating havoc should you have to putt from there. It is a wonderful demanding hole where par is quite an accomplishment.

The next hole gives a little respite to the weary golfer. It's

*OVERLEAF:*
*THE 555-YARD PAR FIVE TENTH, OFFERS A MOST SPECTACULAR VIEW*

a par-three of 203 yards, but the hole goes downhill, usually with the wind at the golfer's back. There are two traps, one small, and one large, with a generous opening between.

Number eight is the first of only two par-fives. It is rumored, that, at 525 yards, it can be reached in two. Tee shots need to be steered to the right side, since the left has mounding that will redirect your ball, as often as not into the rough. The green is behind a bunker with a river bed in front and is fairly flat, thus demanding a high shot. Number ten is the other par five. It is an uphill 555-yard monster that proves a challenge to the best of us. It's a very simple hole as far as strategy goes. Hit it long, and hit it straight. Just in front of the green are three carrot tops of rough, making the chance of running a ball on to the green an improbability.

The ninth hole is a respectable 423 yards long. The second shot to the green has to pass between two large Jeffery pines that resemble goal posts. If you score the field goal, you'll be on a green with three separate tiers. The eleventh hole is 437 yards long and asks for a precise shot off the tee, but it is downhill

and often downwind. The second shot to the green has to go through a narrow opening between the rough on the left and water on the right.

Number twelve is only 321 yards long, but has caused many grimaces and has given birth to many descriptive words, mostly not endearing. You need to respect the golf hole and be secure in your capabilities. Don't hit short and land the shot to the green land on the front; however, landing beyond that will definitely add words to your vocabulary.

The thirteenth fairway has beautiful undulations, with the wind often affecting play. It usually comes from left to right, which is especially important when hitting your approach, which needs to be crisp and pure. The green has two plateaus, with water and sand in front and is about two clubs deep. Number fourteen is a par- three, 190 yards long and surrounded by three bunkers. Putts will break a lot on this green.

The next three holes, fifteen, sixteen and seventeen, dogleg this way and then that, with the bend at seventeen most extreme at almost ninety degrees to the right. To make the tee shot interesting there is out of bounds and wetlands on the right, with the green then tucked behind a bunker.

Number eighteen, is a par-three, a straight shot of about

NUMBER FIVE ABOVE, AND THE EIGHTH FAIRWAY ON THE LEFT

215 yards to a green that has two bunkers on the right, and a larger one behind the green. Sierra Star Golf Course joins other courses, like East Lake in Atlanta and Congressional in Washington, who also have par-three finishing holes.

Designer Olson prides himself on building courses that reflect his philosophy of developing aesthetically pleasing and optimally playing layouts. Golf architects, in order to be competent, have to have an understanding of many disciplines. The first, and arguably the most important, to produce a routing plan that addresses and solves problems. In the case of Sierra Star, the first problem was the existing roads criss-crossing the property. The holes had to be tailored into five separate spaces. A game of Chinese checkers comes to mind.

Another problem was the relative shortage of topsoil and an abundance of boulders. This was solved easily by digging ditches to a depth of fifty feet, producing topsoil, and a convenient place to hide all those rocks—two examples of solving problems with a creative flair.

A golf course needs to seamlessly blend into its surroundings, as if it had been there for eons. This requires an artist's eye and a keen understanding of landscape architecture laced with aesthetics. Contours introduced shouldn't deviate from the existing topography but rather need to blend into it. This takes a touch that is a quality a good architect has to have. Being able to first think in broad strokes and on a moment's notice be obsessed with the detail is another dimension the successful designer must have.

Olson's firm is located in Southern California and, besides Sierra Star, has designed and built many courses around the country and the world. China, Japan, Korea, Taiwan, French Polynesia, Singapore, Mexico, Spain, and Canada are just some of the places where he has created beautiful golf courses for all of us to enjoy.

There is no other sport in which the combatants are so thoughtful, so mindful of their competitors as in golf. This results in one of the happy circumstances the game incorporates. The camaraderie, the friendship, the kinship that percolates between like-minded individuals—it is almost in the mode members of a secret society might behave. You can walk onto any course around the world, join up with a group of players and find instant acceptance, common elation after a good shot and sincere sorrow after a bad one. So it was for me when I played Sierra Star for the first time and joined fellow golfer Chase Foster, a member at the club. He pointed out the dos and don'ts of the course, all the while engaging in light-hearted banter with me. It was a good round of golf made better by the companionship.

John Updike once said: "Golf camaraderie is based on a common experience of transcendence; fat or thin, scratch or duffer, we have been somewhere together where non-golfers never go." Indeed.

T HE SOUTHERNMOST GOLF COURSE ON OUR list is a nine-hole layout presided over by Mammoth Rock. Snowcreek Golf Course was designed by Ted Robinson and is a respectable 6,644 yards long—if you play it twice, that is. There are several sets of tees to choose from, giving the adventurous player a slightly different look when playing the back nine. What remains the same, however, is the grand backdrop of Sherwin Mountain with a rock outcropping, appropriately called Mammoth Rock, that when viewed from certain angles resembles the body of a mammoth. Should you not be able to see the resemblance in the picture to the right, you'll just have to call Gary Paolino, the manager of Snowcreek, and book a tee time and see for yourself. Incidentally, this rock—or should I say the likeness that this rock has to the woolly beast—is not what gave this splendid little town its name. In fact, it's just a happy coincidence, the name

# Snowcreek Golf Course

*6,644 yards, par 70*

*Architect: Ted Robinson*

*Opened for play: 1991*

*Altitude: 7,896 feet*

*Director of Golf: Gary Paolino*

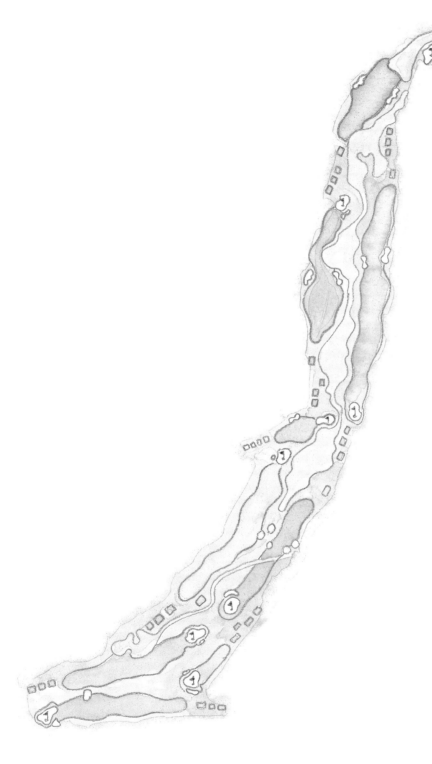

coming from the Mammoth Mining Company which came to this area in pursuit of gold around 1860. When it turned out that there was not enough of the precious metal found to justify operations, the company sold its assets and moved on but left its name.

To the left of Mammoth Rock is what appears to be a ski run. In fact the trees were toppled by an avalanche in 1986 after a three-week-long snowfall. It was named the hundred-year slide, since by coincidence a similar avalanche in the same place slid down the mountain in 1868.

The course is laid out very simply—four holes in one direction, one transitioning, and four holes paralleling the first four coming back. None of the holes bear the usual nine-hole layout curse—short, with no rough on either side of the fairways, no hazards, with greens pancake-flat. These nine holes are all regulation size with all the appropriate accoutrements and not to be challenged with a Sunday bag slung over your shoulder.

Your round starts out on the only par-five, a 569-yard stretch. As will be the case on all other holes, the fairway is not too wide, with traps at the appropriate places. Use them as direction signs and aim to the other side. The second hole, a par four of 416 yards, has a tee shot that starts out over water and has to carry about one hundred and fity yards before reaching the fairway. Number three is a par-three with traps to the side and back. Number four cuts perpendicular to the direction of the previous holes and gets you ready for the return. At 360 yards, it is the only hole that does not have water, but the tee shot has to be launched along a fence that has a ten- or twelve-foot wide apron of native grasses. Your ball is lost should you hit it there. Holes five and six are par-fours, with the 456-yard sixth curling slightly to the left and flanked by home sites. Number seven is a 168 yard par-three with a difficult putting surface. Water is visible on the right but does not really come into play. The lake cuts into the fairway on the 402-yard eighth, setting up a beautiful shot to the green. Similarly, the 398-yard closing hole has an iron shot over water to the green.

Bob Gibson is the greenkeeper. He and his crew of nine are charged with the responsibility of getting the course ready for play in the spring, keeping it in as good a condition as possible during the summer and then getting it ready for "sleep" in the fall. The fall work is probably the hardest and most important. It is the most important because if the greens are not prepared properly, the grass will be disappointing when the snow

THE SEVENTH, A 168-YARD PAR-THREE

melts in the spring. It is the hardest because the tendency is to keep the course open as long as possible, taking a chance with early severe weather. Conditions change quickly in the mountains. For Bob and his crew, it's a constant battle.

The greens, seeded in Penncross bentgrass, are for the most part receptive to iron shots. Some have gentle undulations and some have plateaus that will require the player to get his ball to a specific area, not necessarily the middle of the green. The greens are of moderate size but are large enough to allow

A PANORAMIC VIEW OF SNOWCREEK GOLF COURSE

several hole locations. The fairways are seeded with a mix of Kentucky bluegrass and perennial rye and will offer the player a good lie. The sides are defined either in tall natural grasses or by mounds that are mostly on the right side of the fairway and act as a separator from the adjoining hole going in the opposite direction.

Ted Robinson, the designer, has upward of one hundred and eighty courses that he and his associates have designed or redesigned. Fairbanks Ranch Country Club just north of San Diego and  Ironwood Country Club in Palm Desert are two of his original designs.

Snowcreek Golf Course is one of the few mountain courses in his portfolio, although the course actually occupies a meadow at the foot of the Sherwin Mountains. His design credo is that a course has to be interesting first and then playable for any level of golfer. Finally, it should be in beautiful surroundings. We know that all golf courses are beautiful, some just more so than others. And we all know that a choice of teeing areas and the placement of pins make a course adaptable to many levels of golfers. But interesting? It's a fine line between making a course too hard for all players and making it so easy and straightforward that there is nothing interesting about it.

Mr. Robinson has thoroughly demonstrated his appreciation of these subtleties.

The original design actually was for an eighteen-hole course and was commissioned by Tom Dempsey, the initial owner of the property. For various reasons, some having to do with failed land acquisitions from the U.S. Forest Service, only nine were built. The property is now owned by the Chadmark Group. Luckily, there seems to be a favorable wind blowing to finish the design with a back nine in the near future.

The primary purpose of a golf course, large or small, is for the patrons to enjoy their outing and walk away feeling good, no matter what the score. Judging by the smiling faces leaving the ninth green, more or less everyone who plays this course has a great time, if not a great score.

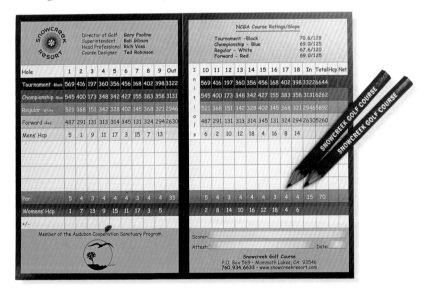

| | Hole | 1 | 2 | 3 | 4 | 5 | 6 | 7 | 8 | 9 | Out | | 10 | 11 | 12 | 13 | 14 | 15 | 16 | 17 | 18 | In | Total | Hcp | Net |
|---|---|---|---|---|---|---|---|---|---|---|---|---|---|---|---|---|---|---|---|---|---|---|---|---|---|
| | Tournament -Black | 569 | 416 | 197 | 360 | 356 | 456 | 168 | 402 | 398 | 3322 | I | 569 | 416 | 197 | 360 | 356 | 456 | 168 | 402 | 398 | 3322 | 6644 | | |
| | Championship -Blue | 545 | 400 | 173 | 348 | 342 | 427 | 155 | 383 | 358 | 3131 | n | 545 | 400 | 173 | 348 | 342 | 427 | 155 | 383 | 358 | 3131 | 6262 | | |
| | Regular -White | 521 | 368 | 151 | 342 | 328 | 402 | 145 | 368 | 321 | 2946 | t | 521 | 368 | 151 | 342 | 328 | 402 | 145 | 368 | 321 | 2946 | 5892 | | |
| | Forward -Red | 487 | 291 | 131 | 313 | 314 | 345 | 131 | 324 | 294 | 2630 | i a | 487 | 291 | 131 | 313 | 314 | 345 | 131 | 324 | 294 | 2630 | 5260 | | |
| | Mens' Hcp | 5 | 1 | 9 | 11 | 17 | 3 | 15 | 7 | 13 | | l s | 6 | 2 | 10 | 12 | 18 | 4 | 16 | 8 | 14 | | | | |
| | Par | 5 | 4 | 3 | 4 | 4 | 4 | 3 | 4 | 4 | 35 | | 5 | 4 | 3 | 4 | 4 | 4 | 3 | 4 | 4 | 35 | 70 | | |
| | Womens' Hcp | 1 | 7 | 13 | 9 | 15 | 11 | 17 | 3 | 5 | | | 2 | 8 | 14 | 10 | 16 | 12 | 18 | 4 | 6 | | | | |
| | +/- | | | | | | | | | | | | | | | | | | | | | | | | |

Director of Golf  Gary Paolino
Superintendent  Bob Gibson
Head Professional  Rich Voss
Course Designer  Ted Robinson

NCGA Course Ratings/Slope
Tournament - Black  70.6/128
Championship - Blue  69.0/125
Regular - White  67.6/120
Forward - Red  69.0/125

Member of the Audubon Cooperation Sanctuary Program

Scorer:
Attest:  Date:

Snowcreek Golf Course
P.O. Box 569 · Mammoth Lakes, CA 93546
760.934.6633 · www.snowcreekresort.com

# Other Golf Courses in the High Sierra

PLUMAS PINES GOLF RESORT    Homer Flint designed this 6,504 yard, par 72 golf course. It opened for play in 1980 and has developed an enthusiastic following to its charms. It starts out in a meadow, then continues through tree lined fairways. For tee times, call: (530) 836-1420

GRAEGLE MEADOWS GOLF COURSE  This is an eighteen hole championship course located along Highway 89 in Graeagle. Most people have a smile on their face when you see them finishing their round on eighteen. The Feather River and the scenic wonders of the Sierra Nevada are a constant companion on your trip around this wonderful golf course. For tee times, call: (530) 836-2323

PONDEROSA GOLF COURSE  Close to the Truckee airport, this nine hole golf course has features that will attract the seasoned and beginning golfer alike. This course was actually built by the people who lived in the area, for their enjoyment. Narrow tree lined fairways on the first few holes give way to a more open setting. A very enjoyable test of golf. For tee times, call: (530) 587-3501

NORTHSTAR at TAHOE  Designed by Robert Muir Graves, the front nine, this eighteen hole championship course hugs the slopes of the Northstar ski area. The front nine play in open terrain resembling links-style golf. The back nine however are situated in tight tree-lined fairways with water hazards on most holes. This golf course is 6,897 yards long. For tee times, call: (530) 562-2490

LAHONTAN GOLF COURSE  This eighteen hole gem, designed by Tom Weiskopf, regrettably is a private course. There also is a par-three nine hole layout on the property.

OLD BROCKWAY GOLF COURSE  This golf course hosted the first Bing Crosby Tournament in 1934. A nine hole course built by Harry Comstock in 1924, the first few holes start sandwiched in between a busy road, and a supermarket parking lot. But you quickly leave for a more pastoral setting of fairways lined by majestic Jeffery pines and views of the mountains and Lake Tahoe. For tee times, call: (530) 546-9909

TAHOE CITY GOLF COURSE  This course opened for play in 1917. Oldest course at the lake, and designed by May Dunn. The course was commissioned by Southern Pacific Railroad as an amenity to their hotel, and opened with only three holes. There ae nine holes today, that can be played a second time for a slightly different game. Seven holes on one side of the clubhouse, sloping up to a hillside, two on the other engulfed by trees. It is a course perfectly suited for family and light-hearted competition. None of the holes are penal, some are quite pretty and all are to be enjoyed. For tee times, call: (530) 583-1516

LAKE TAHOE GOLF COURSE  This is an eighteen hole, par 71 championship course, 6,707 yards long. Located in the Lake Valley State Recreation Area, in South Lake Tahoe. For tee times, call: (530) 577-0788

TAHOE PARADISE GOLF COURSE  An executive course of exceptional beauty, this 4,028 yard, par 66 course opened for play in 1960. Just four miles from South Lake Tahoe, you'll find a golf course with all the amenities, such as a driving range, a pro shop, lessons, etc. For tee times, call: (530) 577-2121

# *Acknowledgments*

I've always felt as somewhat of a parasite when working on projects such as this book. After all, I merely take someone else's creative effort and portray it as best I can. It is with this thought in mind, that I want to thank the following people:

The golf professionals, and some of their associates, who without having assurances of the final outcome of this book, gave their time with much cheer. Bob Hickam from Old Greenwood, Dirk Skillicorn from Coyote Moon Golf Course, Mike Winfield from Tahoe Donner Golf Course, Eric Veraguth from the Resort at Squaw Creek, Cathy Jo Johnson, Angie Rodriguez and Jeff Clouthier at Incline Village Golf Courses, Randy Fox and Steve Seibel at Edgewood Tahoe, Dennis Alexander and Matt Magnotta at Grizzly Ranch Club, Doug Flynn and Craig Pearson at Whitehawk Ranch Golf Club, Peggy Garner at The Dragon at Gold Mountain, Dave Schacht from Sierra Star Golf Club, and Gary Paolino at Snowcreek Golf Course. Thanks very much to all of you.

The men who put ink to paper so to speak, design these golf courses, and then share their thoughts with me. I am grateful to all the golf architects who gave life to these wonderful courses.

To Larry Dennis, whose command of the English language is a reassuring and welcome resource. And Phil Weidinger who helped me without a quid pro quo. Thanks Phil.

Many thanks to Jack Bridge who gave his time as well as valuable information, and finally, the one person who uttered the right words at the most appropriate time, I want to extend a very special thank you to Micah Baker.